How the United States and Japan
See Each Other's Economy

A Supplement
to the Statement

Toward a New International Economic System: A Joint Japanese-American View..............

by the Research and Policy Committee
of the Committee for Economic Development
and Keizai Doyukai

How the United States and Japan See Each Other's Economy

··

An Exchange of Views between the American and Japanese Committees for Economic Development

Isaiah Frank and Ryokichi Hirono

Editors

Committee for Economic Development

Copyright 1974 by the Committee for Economic Development

Library of Congress Catalog Card Number: 74-79476
International Standard Book Number:
   Paperbound ($5.00) 0-87186-326-X
First printing: July 1974
Printed in the United States of America by Georgian Press, Inc.
Design: Harry Carter
Art derived from woodblock illustrations by Hokusai

COMMITTEE FOR ECONOMIC DEVELOPMENT
477 Madison Avenue, New York, N.Y. 10022

Contents

• •

Foreword

· · · · · · · · · · · · · · ·

THIS VOLUME results from a study begun in 1971 by the Committee for Economic Development and its Japanese counterpart group, Keizai Doyukai. It is published as a companion volume to *Toward a New International Economic System: A Joint Japanese-American View*, the statement issued by the two groups as one outcome of their study. The two papers in this volume, which represent the views of each of the participating groups toward economic and social development in the other country, were instrumental in the development of the final policy recommendations agreed upon by the CED Research and Policy Committee and by Keizai Doyukai.

The collaboration of CED and Keizai Doyukai began fourteen years ago and arose out of a deep mutual concern with the role that Japan, then experiencing a burgeoning postwar recovery, would play in the world economy. As noted in the new policy statement, the first focus of interest was the liberalizing of both the economic policies of the major industrialized nations toward Japan and Japan's protective policies toward imports and foreign investment in Japan. These studies led to the publication of the CED policy statement *Japan in the Free World Economy* (1963), which included a parallel statement by Keizai Doyukai. The dialogue between the two groups has continued over a broadening range of issues through participation in joint projects with other foreign counterpart organizations.

When the two groups again came together for full-scale discussions nearly three years ago, the circumstances differed greatly from those of a decade before. The "Nixon shocks" and the first devaluation of the U.S. dollar had just occurred. These were portents of the sweeping changes in diplomatic, trade, and monetary relations that continued as the discussions between CED and Keizai Doyukai proceeded through 1972 and 1973.

The central issue as perceived by CED and so stated in the introduction to our subcommittee's paper in this volume was this:

> In an increasingly integrated world economy, can each nation adequately exercise the degree of national autonomy required to deal effectively with the persistent and complex problems of its own society? Can each nation cope with such domestic problems as unemployment, inflation, structural change in industry, environmental pollution, and shifting values without sacrificing the substantial benefits of increasingly free international flows of goods, services, capital, and technology, as well as equitable access to the world's resources?

> The answer will depend on the vigor and imagination with which the industrial countries approach the restructuring of the international economic system to bring it into accord with today's realities. As two of the largest and most powerful countries, a special responsibility in this task develops upon the United States and Japan.

It was to this issue that the two groups addressed themselves in drafting the policy statement published simultaneously with this volume. As an initial step, each group agreed to draft a parallel study. The CED study consisted of four basic parts: (1) an analysis of the Japanese economy and its social and cultural foundations, with special emphasis on institutional and structural characteristics that condition Japan's external economic behavior; (2) an assessment of Japanese policies and practices in international trade, finance, and investment and their impact on the United States and other countries; (3) an examination of the lessons for the United States to be found in the Japanese experience; and (4) the outlook for Japan's international economic policy for the rest of this decade.

It should be noted that most of the CED study of the Japanese economy was carried out before the October War in the Middle East. Since then, the world has experienced an oil crisis of far-reaching consequences. Tight supplies and rapidly escalating prices of petroleum have invalidated all prior projections of the balance of payments of the industrialized nations. The effects will be particularly profound in Japan, whose dependence on imported petroleum exceeds that of any other major country.

Given the rapidly changing world economic situation, it is obvious that any attempt to anticipate the outlook for the Japanese economy in the remaining years of the decade is subject to a considerable margin of error. It may well be, however, that 1973 marked a turning point from historically unprecedented economic growth and rising trade and payments surpluses. The oil shortage and increases in oil prices late in that year seriously aggravated an imposing set of problems that had already become apparent: soaring prices at home, a rapidly deteriorating balance of payments, and severe constraints on industry arising from intolerable pollution in this congested island nation. How the Japanese economy as a whole will adjust to the new circumstances at home and abroad remains to be seen.

Research was conducted on behalf of the CED Subcommittee on the United States and Japan in a New World Economy by Isaiah Frank, professor of international economics at the Johns Hopkins University School of Advanced International Studies and director of CED's international economics studies. He was assisted by Seong H. Park, member of the CED economics research staff, who was associate project director of the joint studies with Keizai Doyukai. On the Keizai Doyukai side, the research was conducted by Ryokichi Hirono, associate professor of economics at Seikei University in Tokyo.

The collaboration with the Japanese group has also resulted in a second companion volume to the policy statement, entitled *The Japanese Economy in International Perspective*, edited by Isaiah Frank. It presents a series of papers by individual scholars and experts on Japan commissioned in the course of the joint project. These papers, which were discussed at meetings between the two groups and which were particularly helpful to the CED subcommittee, are now in preparation and will be published by Johns Hopkins University Press.

We are grateful to the Ford Foundation for a research grant that helped to finance these studies.

William M. Roth, *Chairman*
Subcommittee on the United States and Japan
in a New World Economy

CED Subcommittee on
the United States and Japan in a New World Economy

KEIZAI DOYUKAI
Japan Committee for Economic Development

Chairman, Board of Trustees and Executive Board
KAZUTAKA KIKAWADA, Chairman of the Board
The Tokyo Electric Power Company, Inc.

Members of Executive Board
HEIGO FUJII, Counsellor
Nippon Steel Corporation

SUMIO HARA, Chairman
The Bank of Tokyo, Ltd.

NORISHIGE HASEGAWA, President
Sumitomo Chemical Co., Ltd.

HIRO HIYAMA, President
Marubeni Corporation

MASARU IBUKA
Chairman of the Board of Directors
Sony Corporation

HIDEO KAJIURA, Advisor
The Industrial Bank of Japan, Ltd.

RYOICHI KAWAI, President
Komatsu, Ltd.

SHOJIRO KIKUCHI, President
Nippon Yusen Kaisha

KIICHIRO KITAURA, President
The Nomura Securities Co., Ltd.

KOJI KOBAYASHI, President
Nippon Electric Co., Ltd.

TAKUJI MATSUZAWA, Deputy President
The Fuji Bank, Ltd.

TATSUZO MIZUKAMI
Senior Advisor to the Board
Mitsui & Co., Ltd.

SHUZO MURAMOTO, Deputy President
The Dai-Ichi Kangyo Bank, Ltd.

MASAKI NAKAJIMA
Chairman of the Board of Directors
Mitsubishi Steel Manufacturing Co., Ltd.

EISHIRO SAITO, Vice President
Nippon Steel Corporation

HARUO SUZUKI, President
Showa Denko K. K.

HIROSHI YAMANAKA, President
The Meiji Mutual Life Insurance Company

SEIICHI YAMASHITA, Managing Director
Keizai Doyukai

Special Committee on Freedom and Order

Chairman
NORISHIGE HASEGAWA, President
Sumitomo Chemical Co., Ltd.

Members
MAMORU ADACHI, President
Kawasaki Kisen Kaisha Ltd.

TAKAKICHI ASO, Chairman
Aso Cement Co., Ltd.

YOSHITOKI CHINO, Deputy President
The Daiwa Securities Co., Ltd.

MORIHISA EMORI, Counsellor
Mitsubishi Corporation

TATSURO GOTO, Executive Vice President
Mitsui & Co., Ltd.

SUMIO HARA, Chairman
The Bank of Tokyo, Ltd.

KOZO HATANAKA, President
Sakai Chemical Industry Co., Ltd.

HIRO HIYAMA, President
Marubeni Corporation

KYONOSUKE IBE, President
The Sumitomo Bank, Ltd.

MASARU IBUKA
Chairman of the Board of Directors
Sony Corporation

KISABURO IKEURA, Deputy President
The Industrial Bank of Japan, Ltd.

ROKURO ISHIKAWA, Executive Vice President
Kajima Corporation

KIICHIRO KITAURA, President
The Nomura Securities Co., Ltd.

KOJI KOBAYASHI, President
Nippon Electric Co., Ltd.

HISASHI KUROKAWA, President
Mitsubishi Petrochemical Company Limited

TAKUJI MATSUZAWA, Deputy President
The Fuji Bank, Ltd.

KUNIO MIKI, Deputy President
Matsuzaka-ya Co., Ltd.

TEIICHIRO MORINAGA

HIROMU MORISHITA, President
Nippon Shinyaku Co., Ltd.

GAKUJI MORIYA, President
Mitsubishi Heavy Industries, Ltd.

SHUZO MURAMOTO, Deputy President
The Dai-Ichi Kangyo Bank, Ltd.

SHUICHI NARUMO, Executive Vice President
Bridgestone Tire Co., Ltd.

KIICHI SAEKI, President
Nomura Research Institute
of Technology & Economics

EISHIRO SAITO, Vice President
Nippon Steel Corporation

TADASHI SAKAYA, President
Daicel Ltd.

HARUO SUZUKI, President
Showa Denko K.K.

TAKEO TAKEDA, Executive Vice President
Onoda Cement Co., Ltd.

SHOICHIRO TOYODA, Vice President
Toyota Motor Co., Ltd.

HIROSHI YAMANAKA, President
The Meiji Mutual Life Insurance Company

HIROKICHI YOSHIYAMA, President
Hitachi, Ltd.

The American View: Japan in a New World Economy

1. Introduction

•••••••••••••••••••••••

THE PURPOSES OF THIS STUDY are to obtain a better understanding of how the Japanese economic system works and how it has affected Japan's external economic behavior, to examine the major elements in U.S.-Japanese economic relations, and to consider the probable trends in Japanese international economic policy over the rest of the decade.

Many Japanese reacted to the "Nixon shocks" of 1971 as signifying the end of an era of close U.S.-Japanese cooperation in political and economic matters. In all three cases—the textile settlement, the surprise announcement of President Nixon's plan to visit China, and the sudden proclamation on August 15, 1971, of the administration's new economic policy—the profound trauma was caused not so much by the substance of what was done as by what the Japanese viewed as the unduly abrupt and unilateral nature of the action on matters so vitally affecting the interests of a close ally. Subsequent developments brought about a substantial relaxation of tensions, but the current world energy crisis threatens to undermine the progress made during the early 1970s on trade and payments matters.

During the reassessment of its postwar relations with the United States, Japan has decided at least in principle on a major shift in domestic priorities away from the production- and export-oriented policies of

3

the past toward the improvement of the consumption and living standards of its people. For the past several years, the government has been paying increasing attention to such long-neglected needs as better housing, public infrastructure, and social welfare as well as coping with the extremely serious problem of environmental pollution.

From the U.S. perspective, the early seventies have also marked a turning point in both foreign and domestic policy. On the international side, the United States is in transition from a period of expanding power and commitments to a period in which it will exert its leadership less directly, as the strength and self-reliance of its allies increase and as international politics continues to move from the simple dynamics of cold war confrontation to a more complex multipolarity. On the domestic side, the new economic policy signified a determination on the part of the United States to get hold of its inflation, even if it involved government controls on wages and prices—measures unprecedented in peacetime. Success in containing inflation was viewed as a prerequisite for stability in the balance of payments as well as for exercising economic world leadership.

All these developments may be expected to have important repercussions on U.S.-Japanese economic relations. They have come at a time when the resolution of our bilateral problems will need to be fit into the broader restructuring of the international economic system required to accommodate the more integrated world of the seventies.

The positions of Japan and the United States in the world economy have changed radically since the late forties and early fifties. At that time, most observers were pessimistic about the future of Japan, a country of large population and sparse natural resources that had suffered major wartime destruction. Despite the impressive pace of postwar recovery, Japan did not regain its prewar level of per capita real income until 1954. Japan's balance of payments remained in deficit until the mid-sixties, contributing to the persistence of a feeling that its rapid economic growth masked a basic fragility in the country's economic situation.

Throughout this period, the United States played a key role in enabling Japan to pay its way in the world. Until 1952, U.S. occupation costs helped to finance Japanese import surpluses; thereafter, American military expenditures added substantially to Japan's foreign exchange earnings. Japan's massive imports of foodstuffs, cotton, and coal benefited from the concessionary terms of America's surplus disposal program or from short- and medium-term Export-Import Bank credits. Japan also became one of the major borrowers from the World Bank, an institution in which the United States has controlled the biggest bloc of votes.

Perhaps of greatest importance was the lead taken by the United States in opening markets to Japanese goods. Not only did the United States become Japan's principal market, accounting for 30 percent of its total exports, but this country pressed others, particularly the Europeans, to open their markets to the Japanese. The United States also became Japan's principal sponsor for membership in the General Agreement on Tariffs and Trade (GATT) and the Organization for Economic Cooperation and Development (OECD). As late as 1962, President Kennedy cited "the need for new markets for Japan and the developing countries" as one of the five fundamental purposes of the Trade Expansion Act.

Japan's rapid progress during the sixties and early seventies is now a familiar story. During the sixties, Japan's exports grew at the rate of approximately 19 percent per year, twice as fast as the rise in world exports; its trade surplus reached $9.0 billion in 1972, and the surplus in its current account was $6.7 billion. As an exporter, Japan ranks behind only the United States and West Germany. During the same period, Japan's GNP increased by more than 11 percent annually, a rate without parallel in world history. Japan has surpassed West Germany as the third largest economic power in the world.

Today, Japan is experiencing its worst economic stress since World War II. The energy crisis, acute shortages of other key materials, a steep rate of inflation, and a slowdown in business are forcing the nation to undertake a thorough review of its economic policies and priorities. The external economic outlook is also uncertain. After five consecutive years of large balance-of-payments surpluses, Japan recorded a deficit of $10 billion in 1973. This sharp turnaround, reflecting greatly reduced trade surpluses and large outflows of long-term capital, occurred even before the recent dramatic increase in oil prices had its impact.

Before the present uncertainties, the prevailing attitude in the United States toward Japan had been a mixture of admiration and irritation: admiration for the phenomenal success of the Japanese economic performance, irritation at what were believed to be unfair Japanese practices that disrupted the smooth functioning of the international economic system by stimulating the sharp penetration of the U.S. market for product after product while maintaining more extensive trade restrictions than any other developed country in the noncommunist world.

The position of the United States in the world has also changed radically in the last two decades. It emerged from World War II as the only major industrial country with its productive capacity and technological base intact. Its competitive position was strong, and the only limitation on its exports was the shortage of dollars in the rest of the world. U.S. monetary reserves were equal to those of the rest of the world combined. Under those circumstances, the United States assumed primary responsibility for the economic viability of Western Europe and Japan as well as for their defense against external aggression.

Although the real GNP of the United States is still the largest in the world, its relative share has declined substantially as a result of much more rapid growth rates in Western Europe as well as in Japan. During the period from 1950 to 1972, U.S. GNP as a percentage of the total GNP of OECD countries declined from 57 to 45 percent; that of the six countries of the European Community (EC) increased from 19 to 27 percent of the total; and Japan's share rose from 4 percent to more than 11 percent. Actually, the shift has been even greater than indicated by these figures when the continued overvaluation of the dollar in 1972 is taken into account.

In virtually every year between 1950 and 1972, the United States ran a balance-of-payments deficit. Although the deficits were welcomed for a number of years as helping to overcome the dollar shortage and aiding the rebuilding of the war-torn world economy, they emerged as a major and intractable problem beginning in 1958. The deterioration in the U.S. trade position in the latter half of the sixties culminated in 1971 in the first trade deficit that the country had experienced in eighty years. In August 1971, the United States was forced to suspend the convertibility of dollar reserve assets held by foreign central banks. In the realignment of exchange rates that took place in December 1971 and again in February 1973, the dollar was devalued on the average by 17 percent and by about 30 percent in relation to the yen. The yen was floated subsequently.

Although the United States still accounts for approximately 40 percent of the production of the noncommunist industrial world, the changes since 1950 signify that Western Europe and Japan have emerged not only as strong competitors in world markets but as major centers of economic and financial power as well. Among the questions raised by the new situation are how the international economic system should be restructured to reflect their enhanced position, and how the costs and responsibilities for defense and for assistance to the developing world should be shared. Military expenditures in 1972 as a percentage of GNP were 6.4 percent for the United States, 3.5 percent for the NATO countries, and less than 0.9 percent for Japan. Official development assistance as a percentage of GNP was 0.29 percent for the United States, 0.34 percent for the Development Assistance Committee (DAC) countries, and 0.21 percent for Japan.

The future external economic relations of the noncommunist world will also be affected by the improved East-West atmosphere. The Soviet Union has shown a major interest in détente for several reasons: the strength and vitality of Western Europe and Japan as well as the formal U.S. commitments to their defense; the achievement by the Soviet Union of strategic nuclear parity with the United States; and the fragmentation in the communist world, particularly the deepening of the Sino-Soviet split. As a consequence, a more complex and diverse set of political and economic relationships are beginning to develop between the principal communist and noncommunist centers of power.

Because of economic complementarities, geographical proximity, and cultural affinity, Japan's trade and other economic relations with China and the Soviet Union will grow rapidly and will undoubtedly outpace the expansion in such relations on the part of the rest of the noncommunist world. But Japan's relations with China will be constrained by the need to take account of the Soviet Union's concern about China's strategic war-making capability. For the foreseeable future, the United States will remain Japan's principal trading partner.

The pull of Japan toward the noncommunist developing countries of Asia has been strong in recent years, but even closer links are likely to develop over the next decade. Not only will Asia grow as a natural trading partner of Japan, but complementarities will be further developed between the need of Japan to invest overseas in order to meet its rapidly expanding raw materials requirements and the need of the developing countries of Asia for capital and technology to exploit their oil and mineral resources as well as to develop the simpler manufacturing industries.

Despite its formal membership in Western economic organizations such as OECD and the Group of Ten, Japan continues to experience sharp discrimination in the markets of Western Europe. The leading EC countries do not in practice accord most-favored-nation (MFN) treatment to Japan but instead use bilateral agreements to govern trade with it. Japan's share of total imports into the EC (excluding trade among EC countries) amounted to only 3.6 percent in 1972 as compared with Japan's share in total U.S. imports of 16.3 percent. Such evidence as is available would suggest that the attitudes underlying this exclusionary policy are still strong in the enlarged European Community.

All three partners in the noncommunist industrial world—the United States, EC, and Japan—stand poised at a critical point in their economic evolution. The crises and tensions surrounding the issues of energy and resources, international monetary relations, and the role of the multinational corporation signify that the end of an era in international economic cooperation has been reached and that the direction in which to go from here has not been quite decided.

The central issue is whether, in an increasingly integrated world economy, each nation can adequately exercise the degree of national autonomy required to deal effectively with the persistent and complex problems of its own society. Can each nation cope with such domestic problems as unemployment, inflation, structural change in industry, environmental pollution, and shifting values without sacrificing the substantial benefits of increasingly free international flows of goods, services, capital, and technology, as well as equitable access to the world's resources? The answer will depend on the vigor and imagination with which the industrial countries approach the restructuring of the international economic system to bring it into accord with today's realities. As two of the largest and most powerful countries, a special responsibility in this devolves upon the United States and Japan.

2. The Domestic Japanese Economic Base

•••••••••••••••••••••••

JAPAN'S REMARKABLE POSTWAR ECONOMIC PERFORMANCE has perplexed and fascinated the Western world. In this chapter, the salient dimensions of Japan's economic growth are looked at briefly and then the factors responsible in terms of the supply of productive resources available to Japan and the principal government policies affecting their use are examined.

SOME DIMENSIONS OF JAPANESE GROWTH

In the aftermath of World War II, Japan's GNP dropped to half the prewar level. Industrial production in particular was affected and amounted to about 30 percent of the prewar figure. Within less than ten years, however, both GNP and industrial production had regained their highest prewar levels.

Beginning in 1955, when the distortions in the wake of World War II and the Korean War had been dissipated, Japan's economic growth outpaced that of all other industrial countries by such a wide margin that it could aptly be described as the "Japanese miracle." The growth of real GNP accelerated from an annual rate of about 9 percent from 1955 to 1960

9

to above 12 percent from 1965 to 1970 (see Table 1). The rate of increase in the last half of the sixties was more than three times the weighted average rate for all other industrial countries.

With a GNP of almost $300 billion in 1972, Japan trailed only the United States and the Soviet Union in terms of aggregate national output. Between 1955 and 1972, per capita income (in current prices) increased from $460 to $2,750, exceeding that of the United Kingdom and Italy.

Along with the rapid growth in Japan's overall GNP, major changes have occurred in its structure of production. Industrial production has expanded about 8.7 times in the past seventeen years, and agricultural production rose about 1.7 times. Japan has developed an extremely diversified manufacturing sector whose production has ranged from the world's largest tankers to cameras, computers, and color television sets, as well as the traditional textiles and souvenir goods. Particularly rapid expansion of output occurred in iron and steel, chemicals, petrochemicals, machinery, and consumer durables. With diversification has come increasing sophistication of product and a predominance of heavy industries (metals, machinery, and chemicals).

The Japanese manufacturing sector is not only diversified but also highly efficient, and the quality of its products is generally excellent. In such areas as steel, shipbuilding, and electronics, its technology is, on the whole, equal to that of any other country. However, in some highly sophisticated items, such as integrated circuits, aircraft, and certain kinds of precision tools, Japan still lags behind the most advanced technology of the United States and Europe. But Japanese industries are nonetheless making rapid technological strides, so that their competitive power at home and abroad continues strong.

Agricultural performance has also exceeded that of the prewar years. Production is becoming more diversified in response to rising demands for meat, vegetables, and fruit. In the growing of rice, which remains the single most important crop, better seed, more fertilizer, and increased use of machinery have substantially increased yields. Despite the high yields per acre, however, labor productivity in agriculture has lagged behind the rapid rise in industrial productivity.

As in most economies that are late in industrializing, Japan had been characterized in the early postwar years by the persistence of a dual structure. A handful of highly efficient modern industries existed side by side with a large number of small-scale, low-wage enterprises in traditional sectors where productivity growth lagged. The gap in productivity levels and wage scales between large- and small-scale enterprises has narrowed

Table 1. GROSS NATIONAL PRODUCT AND GROWTH RATES OF REAL GNP, MAJOR DEVELOPED COUNTRIES, 1955–1973

GROSS NATIONAL PRODUCT *(billions of current dollars at current exchange rates)*						
	1955	1960	1965	1970	1971	1972[a]	1973[a]
Japan	23.9	43.1	88.4	197.2	225.0	299.4	415.7
United States	403.7	511.4	696.3	993.3	1,068.8	1,155.2	1,289.1
France	48.7	61.5	99.9	147.7	162.8	195.9	—
West Germany	42.8	72.5	115.3	187.3	217.4	257.1	—
Italy	24.1	35.1	58.9	93.1	101.6	118.7	—
United Kingdom	53.8	72.4	100.4	122.0	136.7	149.5	—

AVERAGE ANNUAL GROWTH RATES OF REAL GNP *(percent)*						
	1955–1960	1960–1965	1965–1970	1970–1971	1971–1972	1972–1973
Japan	8.9	10.0	12.1	6.3	9.2	11.0
United States	2.2	4.8	3.3	2.8	6.4	5.9
France	5.0	5.8	5.8	5.5	5.4	6.7
West Germany	6.6	5.0	4.8	2.8	2.9	5.3
Italy	5.6	5.3	5.9	1.6	3.2	5.0
United Kingdom	2.7	3.4	2.4	1.6	2.5	5.8

[a]The figures are taken directly from national sources and are not adjusted for conformity with OECD's standard system.

Sources: OECD, *National Accounts of OECD Countries, 1960–1970* (1972); earlier issues of the same title; idem, *Main Economic Indicators* (September 1973); European Communities Statistical Office, *General Statistics*, no. 6 (1973). Growth rates for 1972–73 are estimates given in *The International Economic Report of the President* (February 1974).

substantially, however. Contributing to this trend have been the tightening of the labor supply, the increased availability of funds to smaller-sized enterprises, the dispersion of modern technology throughout the economy, and the rapidly expanding markets that have enabled small-scale enterprises to grow along with larger firms.

Paralleling the sharp rise in GNP has been a dramatic improvement in the material welfare of the Japanese people. Real GNP per capita rose 4.1 times (or 8.7 percent per year) in the period from 1955 to 1972 — the highest rate of increase in the world. The improvement in living standards is reflected in the wide diffusion of consumer goods; the use of television sets, for instance, has become almost universal, and about one-quarter of all families own private automobiles. Yet, the improvement in some fields, such as housing, diet, and social overhead facilities, has lagged as a higher proportion of current income has been allocated to savings and industrial investment than in other countries.

SOURCES OF ECONOMIC GROWTH

Labor Force. Although poor in natural resources, Japan is rich in highly productive manpower. The Japanese people are diligent, skillful, and well educated. Nine years of .education are mandatory, and most children go on to senior high school. A higher proportion of young people go on to college than in most other industrial countries. Educational attainment is the most important means for achieving social and economic advancement in Japan. Most Japanese parents are highly education-conscious, encouraging their children to become better educated than themselves and saving assiduously to meet the rising costs of higher education. All this has resulted in a labor force highly trained in both general and vocational skills and, perhaps equally as important, receptive to learning new skills on the job.

The increase in the supply of labor has also been an important factor in Japan's postwar economic growth. Between 1955 and 1972, employment rose by 27 percent, or 1.4 percent per year. Until the early part of the 1960s, the growth in the labor force was rapid, but it stabilized in the latter part of the decade because of a slower growth of population and a decline in the labor participation rate. The latter is explained by the rise in school enrollment rates and a higher proportion of older people in the population. By the late 1960s, Japan experienced a labor shortage among younger workers and some skilled workers.

Table 2. PRODUCTIVITY GROWTH AND CHANGES
IN UNIT LABOR COSTS,
MAJOR DEVELOPED COUNTRIES, 1955–1972

(average annual rate of change, percent)[a]

	Japan	United States	France	West Germany	Italy	United Kingdom
Output per man-hour in manufacturing						
1955–1960	10.6[b]	1.6	—	—	—	—
1960–1965	8.5	4.3	4.9	6.4	6.8	4.1
1965–1970	13.4	2.0	6.5	5.6	5.3	3.7
1970–1971	3.5	7.1	4.8	4.9	4.3	5.6
1971–1972	10.1	5.3	7.2	7.0	6.9	5.6
Unit labor costs, in national currency						
1955–1960	−1.6	3.4	5.3	2.9	1.9	3.3
1960–1965	4.3	−0.7	3.8	3.0	6.3	2.2
1965–1970	1.6	4.0	3.2	2.6	3.9	3.6
1970–1971	11.7	−0.2	7.2	9.0	13.4	6.8
1971–1972	5.5	1.0	5.0	4.1	6.5	8.3
Unit labor costs, in U.S. dollar basis						
1955–1960	−1.6	3.4	−1.5	2.9	—	3.3
1960–1965	4.2	−0.7	3.8	3.7	6.2	2.1
1965–1970	1.8	4.0	1.0	4.1	3.8	−0.4
1970–1971	15.3	−0.2	7.6	14.3	15.1	9.0
1971–1972	20.9	1.0	14.7	13.5	12.8	10.8

[a] Figures for the 1960–1972 period are based on least-squares trends.
[b] Estimates based on large-establishment data.

Sources: For 1955 to 1960: U.S. Department of Labor, *Handbook of Labor Statistics* (1969); for 1960 to 1972: Patricia Capdevielle and Arthur Neef, "Productivity and Unit Labor Cost in 12 Industrial Countries," *Monthly Labor Review* (U.S. Department of Labor), November 1973, pp. 14–21.

The slowdown in the growth of the labor force was compensated for by a rapid increase in its productivity. Output per man-hour in manufacturing in the period from 1960 to 1972 increased by 11 percent per year, as compared with a 3.0 percent increase in the United States and a 5.7 percent increase in Germany (see Table 2).

Throughout the postwar period, the low-wage agricultural sector served as a vast reservoir of labor that could be drawn upon for the rapidly expanding industrial sector. The massiveness of this shift is best shown by the fall in agricultural employment from 54 percent of total employment in 1947 to 14 percent in 1972. The comparable figures for the United States and United Kingdom, however, are far lower—4 percent and 3 percent, respectively—suggesting that scope still exists for substantial sectoral shifts in Japan. Once Japan's agricultural labor force declines to about 10 percent, however, further shifts are unlikely because an equilibrium may well be reached in terms of income per head in the agricultural and nonagricultural sectors.°

The transfer of labor from agriculture and other low-productivity uses has been accomplished primarily by the movement of young people when they first enter the labor force as school graduates. Almost 90 percent of rural youth have migrated to nearby towns and larger cities for higher-paying jobs.

In addition to the pull of higher wages in high-productivity industries, the government's industrial policy contributed to accelerating the transfer. Factors of production were induced and assisted in various ways to move out of lagging sectors into those that promised greater returns. In this process, millions of workers moved from low-wage and low-productivity agriculture or from small shops and stores into the high-wage and modern industrial sector. Although the scope for shifts in employment may be more limited from now on, it is by no means insignificant, since large manpower reserves still exist in the commercial sector.

Savings and Investment. High rates of savings and investment have been a key factor in Japan's remarkable growth. Expenditures on fixed capital formation accounted for about one-quarter of GNP during the 1950s and about one-third of GNP during the 1960s. This investment ratio exceeded that of any other country. Fixed investment amounted to $100

° Henry Rosovsky, "Japan's Economic Future: An Overview," in Jerome B. Cohen, ed., *Pacific Partnership: United States—Japan Trade* (Lexington, Mass.: Heath, 1972), p. 16.

billion (in current prices) in 1972, a volume second only to that of the United States. Business investment in plant and equipment has been the major component of fixed investment, accounting for about 60 percent of the total (or 19 percent of GNP) during the 1960s.

Contributing to the high rate of business investment have been: the capital requirements for applying the massive imports of new technology from the West; the increasing competition among Japanese entrepreneurs for larger market shares; the low interest rate policy pursued by the monetary authorities; and various fiscal incentives provided by the government to promote business investment at the expense of consumption. Because of the priority accorded to business investment, capital formation in housing and social infrastructure have lagged in relation to needs. Residential construction was only about one-sixth of total fixed investment as compared with one-quarter in Western Europe and the United States. Although the demand for housing has been strong, residential construction in Japan has been deterred by the sharply rising land cost, a limited supply of mortgage loans, and a lag in housing technology.

Government investment in Japan is relatively large compared with other industrial countries and accounted for about one-quarter of total fixed investment in the 1960s. But about one-half of the government investment was for plant and equipment expenditures by public corporations and government enterprises; the social overhead component therefore accounted for a little over one-half of total government investment. With Japan's high population density and increasing urbanization and industrialization, the deficiency in social overhead capital has become a major problem.

As a consequence of the high level of capital formation, productive facilities have been modernized and expanded, productivity per worker raised, production costs reduced, and Japan's competitive position in international markets strengthened. The high rate of investment has naturally resulted in a rapid increase in Japan's capital stock; the private sector's fixed capital stock more than tripled between 1955 and 1970, and that of the government more than doubled.

The public supported the high level of investment by supplying the savings needed to finance it. In the 1960s, household savings were about 19 percent of disposable income, as compared with 12 percent in West Germany and 7 percent in the United States. Most of the savings found their way into banking and financial institutions, which then channeled them into investments in productive facilities. In addition to household savings, the nation's gross savings of course include those originating in the business (depreciation allowances and retained earnings) and government (tax and other revenues minus current expenditures) sectors. The household sector provided one-third; business depreciation allowances, another one-third; and retained earnings of business and government savings accounted for the remainder.

Most impressive of all is Japan's high personal savings rate (19 percent of disposable income), even though its income levels have been below those in most other advanced countries. Among the principal explanations are the Japanese tradition of thriftiness, retirement at age fifty-five on small pensions, the underdeveloped social security system, large bonus payments in the Japanese wage system, limited availability of consumer credit, and the rapidly rising personal income itself.

In the absence of a comprehensive social security system, the individual Japanese must save for old age and unforeseen emergencies. Because of the limited availability of consumer credit, the Japanese also save for housing, consumer durables, and children's education. Owners of small businesses have similar difficulties in borrowing and therefore have an incentive to plow back earnings. The Japanese wage system with its semi-annual bonuses also tends to raise the propensity to save. It has been found that most household savings are made during the months when a bonus is paid.

A significant feature of the personal savings flow in Japan has been the low interest rate earned on most of these funds in banks and trust companies. The rate of inflation (as measured by the consumer price index) exceeded the interest rate paid on average from 1960 to 1972. At the same time, the low real cost of funds borrowed by business firms has been a major factor in Japan's industrial growth.

The Japanese financial system has been an effective intermediary between savers and investors and has contributed to the growth of business investment through its efficient allocation of credit. Despite the high rate of savings out of profits and depreciation allowances, corporate business investment has grown so rapidly as to require external financing largely through borrowings from financial institutions. Although the situation is in the process of change, large firms have typically been heavily in debt; net worth has averaged only about 20 percent of total liabilities. Stock issues have provided only about 8 percent of industrial funds, and bonds even less. Commercial banks have filled the gap by extensive lending, both long and short term, of individual savings held in the form of deposits. They have in turn been supplied adequate reserves by the central bank. Heavy dependence of industry on loans and of banks on the central bank have provided an easy means for the government to influence investment.

Technology. Although Japanese policy has always aimed at fostering the development of indigenous technologies, its postwar innovations were largely dependent upon technology imported from the West, particularly from the United States. Foreign technology was cheap, in part because the costs of financing expensive and commercially risky research and development efforts had been borne by others. The Japanese themselves tended to concentrate on technical innovations with quick commercial application, including the ingenious adaptation of foreign technology through "improvement engineering."

Foreign technology has been obtained almost entirely by licensing or purchase arrangements and technical tie-ins with foreign firms. Only about 5 percent of all imports of technology has involved direct foreign investment, a relationship that has been discouraged as a matter of policy. Between 1950 and 1972, about 11,000 agreements with a duration of more than one year were made for technology imports with a total purchase cost of about $4 billion. For fiscal year 1970 alone, the cost amounted to about $500 million. Although nearly every sector of industry has been involved in these purchases, the distribution by industry has varied with structural shifts in the economy. Of the total number of contracts made between 1950 and 1972, the machinery and chemical industries together accounted for about 50 percent.

Why have U.S. firms been so willing until recently to supply technology to Japanese firms on favorable terms? As long as U.S. firms were limited in their exports to and investments in Japan, licensing was the only remaining way to use the technology to make money. Even if one company carefully guarded its technical know-how, there was always the possibility that its competitors might supply a similar or even superior technology to foreign firms. Moreover, research and development activities by firms in technology-based industries (such as chemicals, electronics, and aerospace) tended to make existing know-how obsolete very quickly. If existing technology was expected to have a short life expectancy, a strong incentive existed to earn as much as possible by selling it to those who could best utilize it, particularly when the marginal cost to the supplier was virtually zero. Some U.S. businessmen see as an additional reason the unwillingness of most American companies to commit themselves to a marketing effort of their own in Japan even if they could obtain Japanese governmental approval of such an effort.

The Japanese government has also played an important role in promoting technology imports on favorable terms. Imports of technology required government approval, and approvals were granted only for those contracts considered vital either to the development of key industries or to the improvement of Japan's balance of payments. Foreign exchange restrictions provided an effective mechanism for controlling the import of technology. Through this apparatus, the government could monitor the possible impact of new products and processes on domestic competition, especially in the small business sector, and ensure that the particular technology selected was indeed the best available in the world as well as reasonably priced. Each proposed contract was carefully studied for its possible effects on both the importing firm and the Japanese economy.

Another significant role played by the government was that of a countervailing power protecting domestic firms that were desperately in need of modern technology and, as a consequence, had weak bargaining power vis-à-vis Western firms. In order to make the assimilation of foreign technology effective and rapid, the Japanese government also provided industries with assistance in various forms, such as import controls, partial exemption from income tax, special depreciation allowances with additional allowances for export expansion, and exemption from tariffs on imported plant and equipment. All these measures were temporary to induce management and workers to make industry self-supporting.

Postwar technological advances have also included considerable improvement and commercial application of Japan's own research and development efforts. Shipbuilding is an outstanding example. Japanese shipbuilding has become preeminent in the world, especially for its immense petroleum and other bulk carriers. Optics, including cameras, binoculars, and electron microscopes, is another field in which expansion has depended primarily on domestically developed technology. Technological adaptation to obtain superior performance has been an important factor in enhancing productivity throughout the industrial sector.

With its educated work force and resourceful management, Japan has been able to absorb new technology promptly and effectively. With the lifetime employment system, labor-saving innovations or changes in product line do not arouse fears of losing jobs.

Other factors also contributed to Japan's success in technological assimilation. The country's physical plant was heavily damaged during World War II, and rebuilding provided an opportunity to utilize the newest methods. Very high rates of capital investment, combined with government-encouraged programs to "scrap and rebuild," provided continuing opportunity to introduce new technology. The very rapid growth of the economy diminished the risks associated with the introduction of new products.

Japan is now in transition from its heavy reliance on the purchase of foreign technology to greater dependence on an indigenous technological effort. Imports of foreign technology have slowed in recent years, both because Japan has achieved technical parity in many areas with other advanced countries and because Western firms have become increasingly reluctant to make technology available on a straight license basis. To an increasing degree, therefore, Japan must rely on its own ability to develop new technologies and new products. Lately, Japan has been steadily increasing its research and development expenditures, although the volume is still low as a percentage of GNP.

Entrepreneurship. Productivity and economic growth depend basically on the efficiency with which an entrepreneur combines factor inputs under a given range of technological possibilities. Although Japanese entrepreneurs have achieved many successes throughout this century, the postwar period has been particularly favorable to the emergence of entrepreneurial talent. As a consequence of the war, the military was discredited as a power elite, and bureaucratic control over economic activities was weakened. The prewar system of close patronage and protection by the government also broke down. These changes allowed much more scope for entrepreneurial initiatives. In addition, many of the rigidities of status and class were wiped away when World War II displaced the old establishment. Business leaders came to be judged less in terms of family and class background and more in terms of demonstrated ability to carry out the innovative and creative functions of management.

GOVERNMENT POLICIES AND INSTITUTIONS

Government-Business Interaction. The Japanese government is much more involved in business decision making than governments of other industrialized market economies. The interrelationships between business and government are close, complex, and extensive. Basic to this relationship is the Japanese government's view of business as a useful and effective arm in accomplishing national objectives in contrast to the arm's-length and even suspicious attitude of the U.S. government toward business. Although on occasion companies have been forced to abide by decisions deemed by the government to be in the interest of the country or industry as a whole, Japanese businessmen and government leaders have generally succeeded in forging unified economic policies as the end product of a process of protracted consultation and consensus building. This process has often been marked, however, by a good deal of strife not only between government and business but among various government departments.

Government officials and business leaders maintain a complex apparatus of interaction involving important government ministers on the one hand and industry or trade associations on the other. On the part of the government, the Economic Planning Agency develops long-range "indicative" plans. Although no legal sanctions exist for their enforcement, the plans represent an effort to define in some detail the direction of the economy that is visualized as most efficient. Specific policies are developed in the various ministries, of which the principal ones are the Ministry of International Trade and Industry (MITI) and the Ministry of Finance. It has been estimated that these ministries maintain over 300 consultative committees in which businessmen and government officials meet to develop specific policies. Quite apart from formal committee meetings, there is also constant informal interaction between businessmen and government officials through an impressive array of clubs and associations where the leaders of Japanese society meet.

The most important mechanism of government-business interaction is the government's "administrative guidance," that is, the varying means of persuasion used by the government to realize the nation's economic goals and priorities. The guidance takes many different forms and can range from a telephone call to the formal licensing of various types of business activity. In addition, the government exerts its influence through a whole range of aids and incentives, including financing, tax concessions, special legislation, government contracts, research and development grants, and other forms of support.

Japanese businessmen are more accustomed than their counterparts in other industrialized countries to working with the government. They have been doing so since the Meiji restoration, when the bureaucracy and the new industrialists formed a close working relationship to foster industrialization and economic development. Businessmen in Japan have come to expect the government to share the risks of industrial expansion and of market development abroad. Government intervention or participation in the decision-making process has been particularly welcomed when, because of antimonopoly constraints, it might otherwise be difficult to reach the industry-wide agreement important to many business decisions.

Some elements of government-business interaction in Japan are also evident in other private enterprise economies of the West. Long-range planning by the Economic Planning Agency is similar to the French system of indicative planning. In a number of West European countries, governments and highly organized business communities also maintain close relations. But what makes government-business interaction in Japan different is the extent and scale of such relations. The special Japanese pattern is rooted in the country's history and culture with its emphasis on the consensual approach and its tradition of government leadership in industrial development.

Fiscal and Monetary Policy. The major goals of fiscal and monetary policy in Japan, as in other market economies, have been economic growth, full employment, and price stability. In the management of these macroeconomic policies, Japan has given top priority to rapid economic growth.

Business cycles in Japan have usually had a course of three or four years. Although the amplitude of fluctuation has been great, recessions have been brief and their overall impact has not been severe. The slowest growth rate in any postwar year was 2.3 percent in 1954, and the annual average of real growth rates for the recession years of 1954, 1958, 1962, 1965, and 1971 was 4.7 percent, better than the long-term growth performance of the U.S. economy for the entire period.

The postwar recessions in Japan have come about largely as policy reactions to a condition of short-run excess demand. The Japanese economy has moved ahead in great spurts: bottlenecks develop; export products are diverted to domestic uses; imports of needed industrial materials and capital goods increase rapidly. The result has been periodic balance-of-payments crises, which have then been attacked by means of restrictive monetary measures. Restrictive fiscal policy has seldom been used for dampening excessive demand. As soon as the balance-of-payments difficulties are resolved, the monetary restraints are removed and rapid growth resumes.

Monetary policy has been highly effective because of the direct relationship between bank loans and business investment. As noted earlier, major business firms are heavily dependent on commercial banks for investment funds, and the banking system is in turn in continuous debt to the central bank for its reserves.

In guiding the lending policies of the commercial banks, the primary tools employed by the Bank of Japan have been discount rate policy and direct credit rationing. Traditionally, the Bank of Japan has been unwilling to raise the discount rate high enough to discourage borrowing in times of excess demand and has preferred to rely on credit rationing. Through its administrative guidance, the Bank of Japan often determines ceilings for lending to individual banks and for loans by the commercial banks to their customers. As the private capital market develops and more direct borrowing by business takes place in that market, this control system may become less effective, but thus far it has been a highly effective means whereby the central bank has guided the lending activity of the commercial banks. The two other instruments of monetary control—reserve requirements and open market operations—are still of minor significance.

Although unemployment has not been serious in Japan, price inflation, as measured by the consumer price index, has been substantially higher than in the United States. Consumer prices rose at an annual rate of about 5.8 percent between 1960 and 1970, reflecting increases mainly in services, agricultural commodities, and goods produced by small manufacturers where wages have risen more than productivity. Japan's wholesale and export prices, however, remained practically level until the mid-sixties and rose only moderately in the late sixties (Table 3).

In addition to the sustained postwar boom, several institutional and structural factors also contributed to the long-run inflationary pressures: the government policy of agricultural price support; import restrictions on many agricultural products; booming land prices under the pressure of rapid urbanization; some sectoral imbalances accompanying rapid overall growth; and a tendency toward equalizing wage increases between large and small enterprises despite persistent differences in productivity growth.

The current inflation in Japan is the highest among the industrially advanced countries. The wholesale price index rose by 29 percent during 1973, and the consumer price index rose by 18 percent. Moreover, the inflationary pressures stemming from last year's oil price increases are just beginning to surface. Curbing inflation thus remains the major task of the government's current stabilization policy.

With regard to policies for long-term growth, Japan has effectively pursued a combination of tight fiscal and easy monetary policy that has encouraged savings and investment at the expense of consumption. The central government has tended to run a surplus on its general account budget, which is then transferred to the capital budget, thus maintaining an overall balance. At the same time, the Bank of Japan has pursued a low

Table 3. COMPARATIVE PRICE PERFORMANCE, MAJOR DEVELOPED COUNTRIES, 1955–1973

(average annual rate of change, percent)

	Japan	United States	France	West Germany	Italy	United Kingdom
Consumer prices						
1955–1960	2.0	2.0	5.9	1.8	1.9	2.7
1960–1965	6.2	1.3	4.0	2.8	4.9	3.5
1965–1970	5.5	4.2	4.3	2.6	2.9	4.6
1970–1971	6.1	4.3	5.6	5.1	4.9	9.4
1971–1972	4.5	3.3	5.8	5.8	5.7	7.0
1972–1973	11.8 (18.1)[a]	6.2 (8.8)[a]	7.1	7.0	10.7	9.3
Wholesale prices of industrial products						
1955–1960	0.2	1.8	5.7	0.7	−0.3	2.0
1960–1965	−0.2	0.2	2.6	1.3	2.2	2.5
1965–1970	1.9	2.7	3.5	1.6	2.6	3.6
1970–1971	−1.1	3.6	2.2	4.6	3.2	7.8
1971–1972	0.8	3.4	4.6	3.2	4.1	7.1
1972–1973	15.1 (29.1)[a]	7.7 (14.8)[a]	14.6	6.7	—	7.3
Export prices[b]						
1955–1960	0.9	1.3	6.6	1.0	−1.6	1.8
1960–1965	−1.8	1.0	1.3	0.5	0.1	1.8
1965–1970	2.6	3.1	3.7	0.4	1.5	4.5
1970–1971	0.7	3.4	5.8	1.6	6.0	7.6
1971–1972	−2.9	3.4	1.1	1.0	1.1	7.1
1972–1973	9.0	15.3	—	—	—	—

[a]The figures in parentheses are percentage increases from December 1972 to December 1973.
[b]Based on export prices in national currencies.

Sources: IMF, *International Financial Statistics* (various issues); and preliminary data for 1973 from national sources.

interest rate policy in combination with credit rationing. In the future, with the much greater emphasis on social infrastructure, the government will no longer be able to rely to the same extent on transfers from the general account budget. The bulk of the funds required for the increase in social investment will be raised by the flotation of bonds.

Several distinctive features of Japan's government expenditure policy may be noted. First, the share of government current expenditures in GNP is much smaller than in other major industrial countries, reflecting low levels of defense expenditures and transfer payments. Defense expenditures in fiscal year 1972 amounted to only 0.9 percent of GNP, or about 7 percent of the general account budget. Japan's social security system was established only some fifteen years ago, and the level of payment is low and the coverage limited. Second, the share of government capital expenditures in GNP has been larger than in the major Western industrial countries. Government investment has accounted for about one-quarter of the nation's total investment and about one-half of the government's total purchases of goods and services. Third, the Japanese government has generally avoided cutbacks in expenditures for stabilization purposes.

Japan's tax revenue (national and local combined) has been relatively low as a percentage of GNP, amounting to 16 percent in fiscal 1972 as compared with about 30 percent for the United States for that year. As in the United States, however, almost two-thirds of Japan's total revenue is accounted for by direct taxes and contributions to social security. The bulk of indirect taxes is derived from a relatively narrow range of commodities: liquor, gasoline, sugar, some important consumer durables, and luxury goods.

The most important function of fiscal policy in maximizing growth has been to allow business investment demand top priority in the allocation of the nation's resources by restricting government expenditures. Government expenditures have been kept stable, the growth-promoting components of public expenditures have been strongly emphasized, and heavy reliance has been placed by the government on its own savings to finance its investment expenditures. At the same time, various tax and fiscal incentives have been provided for business investment, and personal savings have been encouraged by low tax rates on interest and dividends.

Monetary policy has traditionally supported long-run growth by maintaining low interest rates as a stimulus to investment. At the same time, the objective has been to keep the expansion of the money supply sufficiently under control to prevent a rate of inflation that would undermine the confidence of savers.

In the light of the current spiraling inflation, the Japanese government is considering raising interest rates from 7 percent to more than 10 percent in order to provide incentives to savers. To discourage business borrowing, the Bank of Japan has already raised the discount rate six times during the past year.

Industrial Policy. In the Japanese context, industrial policy refers to a complex set of policies concerned with the promotion and protection of economically strategic industries, the adjustment of industrial structure in response to, or in anticipation of, internal and external competition, and the minimization of market disruption and price instability.

Japanese industrial policy is a product of a long tradition of guided industrialization. The Economic Planning Agency develops long-range plans on the macroeconomic level, but the chief architect of policy is the Ministry of International Trade and Industry. MITI plays a powerful and aggressive role by initiating demand-supply studies or action programs for specific industries and by preparing needed aids and incentives. The main policy instruments have included subsidies, development loans, fiscal incentives, government purchasing, regulatory measures, import controls, restrictions on capital flows, and the sanctioning of various types of cartel arrangements.

The essential feature of Japanese industrial policy has been the strategy of selecting a small number of industries that are deemed to be strategic and of concentrating promotional aids on them. The selection has shifted with the stages of industrial development toward industries of increasing sophistication.

At the end of World War II, when Japan was confronted with the need for economic reconstruction and rapid industrialization, the government targeted five basic industries as strategic: iron and steel, shipbuilding, coal, power, and fertilizer. These industries laid the foundation for the subsequent development of a highly diversified industrial economy. Later, government policy concentrated on developing the metal, machinery, and chemical sectors. It was widely believed that these industries would promote rapid productivity gains through technological innovations, the growth of related industries, and the advance of Japanese exports in international markets. In the 1960s, the industrial structure of Japan shifted rapidly toward heavy and chemical industries, thus catching up with the pattern of advanced industrial economies.

Japan's industrial policy has created a serious reaction among foreign competitors. Continued support of targeted industries through government measures implies interference with free market forces and creates distortions in the conditions of international competition. The situation has been accentuated by a government-business policy of maintaining continuing industrial growth in spite of domestic recessions through temporary increases in an already aggressive export drive. There is a growing feeling among Japan's trade partners that the strategy of target industries combined with aggressive export promotion measures frequently result in cutting into competitors' exports to third countries as well as market disruptions in the importing countries.

Japan's present industrial policy is to promote the development of knowledge-intensive industries such as computers, oceanography, medical equipment, fashion, and leisure. The new policy will also give priority to infrastructure, housing, pollution control, and social welfare facilities. Traditional labor-intensive and raw-material processing industries are being de-emphasized. The new policy is much wider in scope and involves many more private interests and government agencies than the previous key-industry policy. There is more to coordinate because of the wider range of structural problems and the economy's expanded size. Although a broad consensus exists on the long-term policy direction, actual implementation of the new industrial policy is bound to pose serious difficulties over the years ahead.

Agricultural Policy. Agriculture in Japan epitomizes in extreme form many of the problems and contradictions facing this sector in most of the countries of the industrial world. Japanese farming is a small-scale enterprise, but it is a highly productive one. The average farm is only 2.7 acres, as compared with 26 acres for West Germany, 78 acres for the United Kingdom, and 290 acres for the United States. Between 1950 and 1968, aggregate agricultural output expanded at about 3.8 percent annually as compared with the prewar growth rate of about 1 percent. Since 1969, the growth rate has slowed somewhat due to a decline in rice output. As a result of expanded investment and improved technology, the productivity of agricultural workers has almost doubled in ten years, and farm incomes have substantially increased. Because of the more rapid increase in industrial production, however, agriculture's contribution to domestic product has steadily declined, from 16 percent in 1955 to 5 percent in 1970.

Rice has been Japan's major agricultural product, but there has been a shift of production within agriculture reflecting rising incomes and changes in consumption toward high-protein diets. The share of rice in total agricultural output declined from 48 percent in 1960 to 38 percent in 1970; whereas the shares of livestock products, fruits, and vegetables have increased substantially.

As in other industrial countries, labor has been moving steadily out of agriculture into higher-growth areas, primarily manufacturing industries. Between 1960 and 1970, the labor force in agriculture declined from 12 million (27 percent of the total working population) to 8 million (15 percent of the total working population). Only 30 percent of those remaining are males under sixty years of age, and a large part of the income of farmers is earned from other employment. Farmers still have considerable political power, however, due to their disproportionate representation in the Diet. But despite rising consumer discontent with high food prices and the obvious need for increased imports, the government continues to support some 70 percent of agricultural production at prices well above the world market.

Until 1960, the price of rice was kept in line with general price increases under a parity price formula. This situation changed, however, with the introduction of a new formula in 1960 designed to achieve income and wage parity between farmers and urban workers. With this formula, the government purchase price of rice rose rapidly, more rapidly in fact than the rise in industrial wages. It more than doubled between 1960 and 1968, and by 1970 the domestic price of rice stood at twice the import price. Surplus rice in government storage reached 8 million tons in 1971. The goal of reducing the gap between farm and nonfarm income was thus sought through rising prices.

Adoption of the income parity objective under the new formula imposed a heavy burden on taxpayers and involved substantial loss of economic efficiency. Government expenditures for agricultural support amounted to $1.3 billion in fiscal 1971, or 5 percent of the total national budget. The price support policy hindered the shift of agricultural resources from rice production to other products of increasing demand such as livestock and vegetables. As a result, the prices of the latter have risen sharply in recent years, contributing to the increase in overall consumer prices.

Because of the rising burden of the rice control program and the ever-increasing rice surplus, the government froze the purchase price in 1968 and subsequently launched a program for the retirement and diversion of paddy fields. After a two-year freeze, however, the government yielded to pressure from the farmers and raised the purchase price (in

1971 and 1972), although at a much-reduced rate of increase. However, in 1971, the government set the limit on its purchase of rice at 5.8 million tons while allowing farmers to sell part of their rice to other buyers. These steps represented a reversal of the past policy of government purchase of rice in unlimited quantities. In 1973, the government again switched its policy to encourage production. It raised the purchase price for rice by a record 16 percent and decided to terminate acreage limitations on rice.

The Japanese government maintains a variety of restrictions against agricultural imports. About twenty products (including rice, wheat, flour, barley and other grains, beef, milk and cream, processed cheese, oranges, and fruit juices) are under quota restrictions, accounting for the major share of Japan's remaining import quotas. In addition, processed farm products are subject to relatively high import duties. As a result of this agricultural protection, Japan's dependence on imported foodstuffs has been low; its ratio of imported foodstuffs to consumption was 7.3 percent in 1969, as compared with 28.4 percent for the United Kingdom and 10.3 percent for France and Italy for the same year.

Both domestic consumers and Japan's trade partners have been pressing for the liberalization of agricultural imports. Some of the major items of interest to the United States are beef, fruit juices, and oranges. When the import quota on grapefruit was lifted in June 1971, Japan's imports of that product increased about fivefold despite a high tariff. It is clear that the Japanese market can and should absorb a great deal more of American farm products, despite the doubts about relying on U.S. sources of supply caused by the recent temporary American export restrictions on soybeans and other agricultural products.

Reorganization of small and fragmented farms into larger and more economic units is the most intractable of all Japanese agricultural problems. Although record yields per unit of land have recently been achieved, the rise in output per man has not been rapid enough to keep pace with productivity in manufacturing. Consolidation of small holdings into more economic-sized holdings is a prerequisite to further mechanization and higher productivity in Japanese agriculture. With the ongoing outflow of labor from agriculture, it was hoped that existing farmland would pass into the hands of full-time farmers, thus enlarging the scale of the remaining farms. Instead of selling their land, however, many owners have remained part-time farmers, with the result that the small size of the average Japanese farm has persisted despite the substantial outflow of labor.

A number of factors have accounted for the failure of government policy to attain its objective of structural improvement. Rising land prices make land an excellent store of value, and owners are hesitant to sell, anticipating a further increase in price. On the other hand, few potential buyers are willing to buy the land for agricultural purposes at a price that is uneconomic for farming. Furthermore, the heavy capital gains tax serves as a disincentive to the sale of farms. Another reason for holding on is the inadequacy of old-age pensions. Many part-time farmers retain their farm so that upon retirement, they can have a place to live and grow at least a minimum of food for themselves.

The Japanese government is aware of these problems and has taken several steps aimed at the consolidation of farming units. An old-age pension system for farmers has been established to encourage older farmers to retire and leave the farm. Limitations on the maximum acreage for individual landholding have been raised, and restrictions on land leasing have been relaxed. Finally, the government is providing financial and technical aids for the formation of agricultural cooperatives.

MARKET ORGANIZATION AND COMPETITION

Japan has taken a rather pragmatic approach toward the problems of industrial organization, concentration, and restrictive practices. The pattern of market organization that has emerged in postwar Japan has been characterized by keen rivalry among large firms on the one hand and various types of collusive actions on the other. Mergers, industrial reorganization, and cartels have often been encouraged on the ground that such actions contribute to eliminating "excessive competition" while improving Japan's competitive position in the world economy.

Japan's basic law on competition and restrictive practices is its Anti-Monopoly Act enacted in 1947. It was modeled after the U.S. antitrust statutes and aimed at establishing a competitive business environment and preventing the concentration of economic power. In order to administer the act, a Fair Trade Commission (FTC) was established. Through successive revisions in 1949 and 1953, however, the original act was modified to allow mergers, cartels, and other forms of "cooperative" arrangements to be created more easily as a means of achieving economic stability and a more rational use of resources.

Although Japanese leaders subscribe to the ideology of free competition, they have in practice promoted cooperation among business firms and between business and government. High priority is placed on maintaining harmony within an enterprise as well as with other enterprises. Government policy reflects a good deal of concern with the cost of a competitive system, that is, cyclical fluctuations and overcapacity in specific industries.

Major industries in postwar Japan have been divided into hierarchical groups (keiretsu), each consisting of a major bank or banks and a number of large firms closely affiliated with it. Each large firm in turn is tied to a set of small subcontracting firms. Unlike the prewar situation, the present system of business groupings is more pluralistic and loosely linked through cross-holdings of each other's stocks. There are no holding companies such as those that controlled the prewar zaibatsu system, although banks within each affiliated group have assumed the unifying role that prewar holding companies played. Each of the major business groups has a council of chief executives that meets regularly and attempts to coordinate the policies of member firms. The banks have played a central role in strengthening the competitive position of member firms of each business grouping by financing aggressive expansion, by encouraging diversification, and by promoting various forms of cooperative action, including mergers.

This system has tended to encourage a high degree of concentration of capital, but the large firms nevertheless engage in keen competition for market shares through aggressive investment in new plant and equipment and active introduction of new technology. When the economy grows year after year by 10 percent in real terms, the test of a company's performance is its market share. This type of competitive mechanism has frequently resulted in overexpansion of capacity and strong pressures to dispose of goods at reduced prices in foreign markets.

Mergers have become an increasingly important avenue to market concentration in the Japanese economy. Under the Anti-Monopoly Act, a merger requires advance approval by the FTC in order to ensure against a substantial restraint of competition. Nevertheless, mergers took place at an annual rate of 300 to 500 in the 1950s and of more than 1,000 in the 1960s. Whereas earlier mergers were mostly among smaller enterprises, recent mergers have included a substantial number of consolidations of large firms. The most celebrated recent case was the merger in 1970 of Japan's two largest steel companies (Yawata and Fuji) into Nippon Steel, which then became the largest steel company in the world.

MITI has encouraged mergers and industrial reorganization as a means of achieving economies of scale, preventing redundant investment, and eliminating excessive competition. The FTC has generally accepted the reasoning of MITI and approved most merger plans. But the commission has repeatedly pointed out the danger of price rigidity resulting from increased concentration and has urged safeguards against oligopolistic pricing practices. MITI officials, on the other hand, contend that this danger must be tolerated because the increase in size of firms is desirable in the interest of international competitiveness.

Japanese government policy toward cartels and other collusive actions has also been highly flexible. Although the Anti-Monopoly Act originally prohibited cartels, subsequent amendments and new legislation permit cartels under a variety of circumstances.

Depression cartels may be allowed by the FTC when the price of a commodity is under pressure and a substantial number of firms in an industry face the threat of bankruptcy. A depression cartel may comprehend the curtailment of investment, production, or sales as well as price-fixing. In general, such cartels have been of brief duration because they have been organized for the purpose of restricting output during recession.

Rationalization cartels are permitted when agreements among firms are deemed necessary in order to promote technological advancement, improve the quality of products, or reduce cost. In addition to agreements on technology, rationalization cartels may provide for the joint purchase of raw materials or joint use of storage and transport facilities. They may not, however, restrict output or fix prices.

Foreign trade cartels are exempt from the application of the Anti-Monopoly Act but are regulated by the Export-Import Transaction Law, which, as of March 1971, had authorized nearly 200 such cartels. The agreements may cover prices, volume of exports, design, or other conditions. Some of the "voluntary" export restrictions (imposed at the explicit request of an importing country) are carried out through foreign trade cartels sanctioned under this law.

The Small Enterprise Cooperative Law provides the legal basis for a variety of collective actions on the part of small firms. Cartels and cartel-like practices are among the sanctioned activities.

As important as the legally sanctioned cartels have been the advice cartels formed under the administrative guidance of MITI. Under an advice cartel, MITI makes recommendations regarding production quotas, floor prices, restrictions on investment in equipment, or the freezing of inventories. Actual implementation of the cartel arrangement is typically left to the industry itself.

The proliferation of mergers, cartels, and similar arrangements has stimulated searching questions on the present state of Japan's antitrust policy. Criticism has been directed at both antimonopoly policies in general and specific mergers and cartels. An important aspect of the criticism is that whereas cartels and other restrictive arrangements have been effective in fixing prices and limiting output, they have failed to prevent the growth of excess capacity. As a consequence, a demand has arisen for more effective cartels, and firms have come to depend on them. With sales at artificially high prices at home and low prices abroad, a double reaction has set in. On the one hand, the voice of the Japanese consumer is increasingly being heard in opposition to practices for which he bears the domestic cost. On the other hand, the charge of dumping has increasingly been leveled against Japanese firms by their competitors abroad. As U.S. antitrust laws and court decisions have been heavily adverse to price discrimination, Japanese firms trading in the United States face large risks in maintaining unjustifiable disparities between domestic and foreign prices or in prices charged in different foreign markets.

LABOR-MANAGEMENT RELATIONS AND THE EMPLOYMENT SYSTEM

Labor-management relations in Japan have rarely taken the form of confrontations so common in other industrial countries. Japanese labor unionism consists of enterprise-wide or plant-wide unions, which constitute the actual bargaining units; the nationwide unions are associations of independent enterprise unions. An enterprise union is organized primarily among the regular employees of a firm, and its very existence depends on the survival and growth of the firm. As a result, the bargaining power of an enterprise union is limited. Its primary concern is job security rather than wage maximization. Strikes have been few, brief, and symbolic. Labor days lost have been minimal, and output foregone has been small.

It would be a mistake, however, to view the placid state of labor-management relations in Japan as entirely a result of special institutional factors. Wage rates in manufacturing have been increasing in recent years at about 16 percent annually in real terms. Should the growth in industrial output and therefore in real wages slow down substantially, prolonged and serious strike interruptions may well occur.

The institutional mechanism for wage determination in Japan centers on the negotiation of a wage contract between a company and its union carried out once a year. The importance of these Spring Round wage negotiations has been growing from their inception in 1955. Each year, the majority of organized workers takes part in the March-to-May round. The union's normal practice is to demand a higher base-up than the one obtained in the previous year. The base-up covers all the regular contractual elements of wage earnings of workers already on the payroll. It includes wage increases that would have taken place automatically, notably on account of length of service, but excludes overtime and bonus payments. Each year's base-up is roughly equivalent to that of the previous year plus an amount directly linked to the profits of large enterprises. Certain industries often set a pattern of wage increases during the Spring Round, which is then followed to a greater or lesser extent in other sectors.

This spring's wage negotiation is attracting particular attention because of its possible impact on the wage-price spiral. Labor unions are demanding extremely large wage increases this year (more than 30 percent) to protect their incomes from the country's worsening inflation. Despite the government's pleas for self-restraint, labor shows few signs of yielding. Prices continue to rise in the face of a series of restrictive financial measures. Increasing sentiment is developing for an income policy to mitigate the serious cost-push pressures.

The Japanese employment system, although under some stress, remains predominantly one of lifetime employment, with compensation primarily determined by age, length of service, and education. This system does tend to reduce job mobility and to breed a feeling of complacency among employees, but it has important advantages from the point of view of resource allocation. It provides a stable and dependable work force, and it rewards fast-growing companies and industries while penalizing slow-growing ones. (The former are able to recruit a large number of new and young workers with lower starting wages, with the result that average costs in these firms become lower than in the latter group.) Also, the costs of labor unrest and strikes are minimized, and the introduction of new technology is prompt and frictionless.

The lifetime employment system in Japan also makes labor more a fixed than a variable cost. Since a high fixed cost is imposed by a heavy dependence on bank loans for capital funds, the cost of material inputs is the only remaining variable cost. The high ratio of fixed costs places a tremendous premium on a full-capacity production policy. In times of recession, management often maintains prices at home through recession cartel agreements while ensuring continued full operation by selling abroad at prices covering little more than variable costs. If such practices are followed in sales to the United States, as noted above, application of antidumping or antitrust laws is highly probable.

CURRENT CHANGES IN PRIORITIES

Until the late 1960s, Japan was preoccupied with promoting rapid growth and improving the competitive strength of its industries in international markets. But Japan's success in achieving these objectives was won at the cost of serious economic and social imbalances. Social overhead facilities and welfare services have lagged behind the growth of income; housing standards remain inadequate; problems of urban congestion and industrial pollution have become acute.

The oil crisis struck just at a time when the Japanese government was beginning to pay increasing attention to the need to achieve a pattern of economic growth that contributes more directly to higher consumption and an improved quality of life, with less emphasis on industrial investment and exports. Priorities in the allocation of resources were being shifted to social infrastructure, housing, social security, urban improvement, and the control of environmental deterioration. Although the oil crisis lends additional weight to the case for this shift in priorities, it also affects Japan's ability to carry it out.

Japan now finds itself constrained by reduced supplies and rising prices of resources that must be obtained abroad. These changes have exacerbated domestic inflation, weakened the competitiveness of Japanese goods, and reduced the country's growth potential. But the past record demonstrates the resiliency and flexibility of the economy and its ability to achieve stated goals once a consensus is reached. Under the new conditions, Japan's growth rate will undoubtedly decline from the level of the past decade, but it may continue to remain very high by Western standards.

3. Trade Performance and Policy

• • • • • • • • • • • • • • • •

THE FORCES UNDERLYING THE RAPID GROWTH of the Japanese economy also strengthened its competitive position internationally and had a profound impact upon trends and patterns of foreign trade. In 1955, Japan's exports accounted for 2.1 percent of total world exports; by 1972, the figure had more than tripled, reaching 7.1 percent. During this period, Japanese exports grew at a rate of approximately 17 percent per year, more than twice as fast as the growth of world exports. Japan's export growth accelerated in the late 1960s, when the annual increase exceeded 20 percent. By 1972, exports reached $28 billion, making Japan the third largest exporter after the United States and West Germany (see Table 4).

Japanese imports also expanded rapidly, but at a slower pace (14 percent per year) than exports. The Japanese share of world imports grew from 2.5 percent to 5.6 percent in the period from 1955 to 1972. In 1972, total imports amounted to $19 billion (f.o.b.). With the more rapid growth of exports, Japan became a country of ever-increasing trade surplus, which by the end of 1972 amounted to $9 billion.[*]

---

[*] Unlike U.S. practice, imports by Japan are normally expressed in c.i.f. terms. On that basis, imports in 1972 were $23 billion, and the trade surplus was $5 billion.

In 1972, however, Japan's export growth began to lag behind that of its major European competitors; and by 1973, it fell behind the rate of increase of U.S. exports as well. Moreover, Japan's export growth lagged far behind that of its imports in 1973, resulting in a sharp reduction of its trade surplus (on an f.o.b. basis) from $9 billion in 1972 to less than $4 billion in 1973.

Several factors were responsible for this turnaround in Japan's trade position: the cumulative revaluation of the yen since 1971; export-restraint and import-liberalization measures adopted during this period; strong domestic demand during 1973, which reduced export capacity and stimulated demand for imports; and rapidly rising import prices of oil and other materials.

COMMODITY COMPOSITION

Japan is unique among today's large industrial countries in the degree to which its exports are concentrated in manufactured products and its imports in raw materials. As early as 1955, manufactures had accounted for 87 percent of total exports, but this proportion grew to 96 percent by 1972. Foodstuffs, mainly fish and vegetable preserves, account for most of the remainder. Japan's export surplus in manufactured products alone increased from less than $1.5 billion in 1955 to some $20.4 billion in 1972 (f.o.b.-c.i.f.).

The most dynamic commodities in Japanese exports in this period were the products of heavy industry: metals, chemicals, and machinery. Their share rose from about 33 percent of total exports ($660 million) in 1955 to 77 percent ($20.1 billion) by 1972. Exports of light manufactured goods, which made up about half of the total in 1955, lagged behind, their share declining to about 19 percent in 1972. Textiles, which had accounted for nearly 40 percent of total exports in the early 1950s, declined to 10 percent in 1972. The products of heavy industries have thus replaced textiles as the leading export items. In 1972, Japan's principal exports were iron and steel, ships and boats, motor vehicles and motorcycles, television and radio receivers, synthetic fabrics, tape recorders, scientific and optical goods, and clothing.

In contrast, about two-thirds of Japanese imports consist of raw materials and food. Imports of fuels and ores in particular have risen rapidly in the past seventeen years. The proportions of food and agricultural raw materials, however, have declined somewhat, partly because of an increas-

Table 4. EXPORTS AND IMPORTS OF SELECTED COUNTRIES, 1960–1973

EXPORTS (f.o.b.) (billions of current dollars)

	1960	1970	1971	1972	1973
Japan	4.0	19.3	24.0	28.6	36.9
United States	20.4	43.2	44.1	49.8	71.3
France	6.9	17.9	20.8	26.5	36.6
West Germany	11.4	34.2	38.9	46.7	67.5
Italy	3.6	13.2	15.1	18.5	—
United Kingdom	10.2	19.3	22.3	24.3	30.5

AVERAGE ANNUAL GROWTH RATES OF EXPORTS (percent)

	1950–1960	1960–1970	1970–1971	1971–1972	1972–1973
Japan	15.9	17.5	24.4	19.2	29.0
United States	5.1	7.7	2.1	12.9	43.2
France	6.4	9.7	16.2	27.4	38.1
West Germany	16.6	11.2	13.7	20.1	44.5
Italy	10.5	13.9	14.4	22.5	—
United Kingdom	4.8	6.0	15.5	9.0	25.5

IMPORTS (c.i.f.)[a] (billions of current dollars)

	1960	1970	1971	1972	1973
Japan	4.5	18.9	19.7	23.5	38.3
United States	15.1	39.9	45.6	55.6	69.1
France	6.3	19.1	21.3	27.0	37.7
West Germany	10.1	29.8	34.2	40.2	55.0
Italy	4.7	15.0	16.0	19.3	—
United Kingdom	12.6	21.7	23.9	27.8	38.9

AVERAGE ANNUAL GROWTH RATES OF IMPORTS (percent)

	1950–1960	1960–1970	1970–1971	1971–1972	1972–1973
Japan	12.1	14.3	4.2	19.3	63.0
United States	4.9	11.3	14.3	21.9	24.3
France	5.7	11.5	11.5	26.8	39.6
West Germany	13.3	10.5	14.8	17.5	36.8
Italy	9.1	11.0	6.7	20.6	—
United Kingdom	3.7	5.8	10.2	16.3	39.9

[a] U.S. imports are in f.o.b. values.

Sources: UN, *Handbook of International Trade and Development Statistics* (1972); and IMF, *International Financial Statistics* (March 1974).

ing degree of self-sufficiency promoted by the government in several basic foodstuffs and the substitution of processed industrial materials for primary products. Principal imports in 1972 were crude petroleum, lumber, iron ore and scrap, nonferrous ores, coal, raw cotton, soybeans, wheat, sugar, and wool.

Although the share of manufactured goods in total imports has risen considerably in the 1960s, the level of such imports has remained relatively low. The increase has been largely concentrated in machinery and equipment needed for the modernization of domestic industries. Imports of manufactured consumer goods have also risen slightly, but their share remains very low as compared with other industrial countries.

GEOGRAPHICAL DISTRIBUTION

The geographical distribution of Japanese exports has undergone considerable change in the postwar period. Exports to developed countries rose much more rapidly than exports to developing countries, but the rise in the share of the former was largely the result of a steady increase in the U.S. share (see Table 5). The United States has been Japan's principal export market, its share increasing from 22 percent in 1955 to 31 percent in 1972. Although Japanese exports to Western Europe and Oceania also rose, their shares remained relatively small.

Japan's second most important export market has been the countries of Southeast Asia. Although the relative importance of this group as a whole has declined (from 37 percent in 1955 to 22 percent in 1972), a number of countries within the area (Korea, Taiwan, Hong Kong, Thailand, and Singapore) have absorbed a rising proportion of Japanese exports. Japanese exports to the Sino-Soviet bloc increased significantly during the 1960s, but they still represent only a small proportion of Japan's total exports.

In comparison to Japan's export market, the geographical origins of Japanese imports have undergone fewer marked changes since 1955. Throughout the period, the United States has been the largest single supplier, but its share in Japan's total imports has declined since 1970, in contrast to the steadily increasing U.S. share of Japan's exports. Among the developing countries, the Middle East's share rose rapidly because of Japan's increasing imports of oil. The weight of Southeast Asia, on the other hand, declined considerably partly because of Japan's increasing self-sufficiency in food production.

Table 5. GEOGRAPHICAL DISTRIBUTION OF JAPAN'S FOREIGN TRADE, 1955–1972

EXPORTS (percent)						
	1955	1960	1965	1970	1971	1972
Developed countries	45.0	47.6	50.9	54.0	54.2	55.8
United States	22.3	27.4	29.3	30.7	31.2	30.8
European Community	4.0	4.3	5.7	6.7	6.8	7.7
United Kingdom	3.0	3.0	2.4	2.5	2.4	3.4
Developing countries	53.5	50.6	43.4	40.5	40.9	39.2
Southeast Asia	37.0	32.3	26.0	25.4	24.0	22.1
Communist countries	1.4	1.8	5.7	5.4	4.8	5.0
Mainland China	1.3	0.2	2.9	2.9	2.4	2.1
Total	100.0	100.0	100.0	100.0	100.0	100.0

IMPORTS (percent)						
	1955	1960	1965	1970	1971	1972
Developed countries	51.0	56.8	51.2	55.2	52.1	52.5
United States	31.3	34.6	29.0	29.4	25.3	24.9
European Community	3.5	4.7	4.8	5.9	5.8	5.9
United Kingdom	1.5	2.2	3.7	2.1	2.1	2.1
Developing countries	45.4	40.3	42.3	40.1	43.1	42.2
Southeast Asia	26.9	19.6	17.2	16.0	17.3	17.8
Communist countries	3.6	2.9	6.5	4.7	4.8	5.2
Mainland China	3.3	0.5	2.8	1.3	1.6	2.1
Total	100.0	100.0	100.0	100.0	100.0	100.0

Sources: Bank of Japan, *Balance of Payments Monthly;* and UN, *Direction of International Trade* (for 1955 and 1960).

FACTORS CONTRIBUTING
TO JAPAN'S EXPORT GROWTH

Among the principal factors contributing to Japan's remarkable export performance has been the rapid absorption of new technology that made Japanese products highly competitive in terms of price and quality. Increasingly, Japanese exports have concentrated on such commodities as iron and steel, machinery, and motor vehicles, where cost-reducing technological progress has made its largest contribution.

The massive absorption of technical and organizational progress as well as increases in capital per worker have made it possible for Japan to achieve the world's most rapid rise in output per man-hour in manufacturing. The average increase in productivity in manufacturing between 1960 and 1972 was about 11 percent per year, as compared with about 6 percent in West Germany and 3 percent in the United States. As a consequence, a rapid rise in Japanese wages could be sustained without appreciable cost and price increases.

Stability in export prices has been an important source of competitive advantage for Japanese exporters. Although domestic consumer prices rose about 76 percent (5.8 percent per year) between 1960 and 1970, the increase in export prices was very small, about 0.5 percent per year. For many commodities, export prices actually declined.

Also contributing to Japan's export performance was a carefully articulated industrial policy through which the government developed and rationalized certain industries while phasing out others. A major priority in the industrial policy has been the desire to improve the country's export capacity. Government policies to promote exports included credit at preferential rates, tax incentives, extraordinary depreciation allowances for exports, and support for export cartels that allowed integrated and cooperative programs for the penetration of foreign markets.

ROLE OF TRADING COMPANIES

The bulk of Japanese foreign trade is carried out through trading companies (shoji kaisha), which have played an important role in Japan's export success. The Japanese trading company is a highly efficient channel for export marketing as well as a dominant element in the nation's internal distribution system. Japanese manufacturers, both large and small, rely heavily on the general trading company for marketing their products.

Some very large business groups, such as Mitsui and Mitsubishi, have their own trading companies to which they delegate the whole of their sales activities. A trading company frequently buys a product from a small manufacturer and puts its own name on it, thus accepting responsibility for the product, including after-sales service. Trading companies have permanent offices in all major commercial centers of the world, where they keep continuously in touch with market conditions and buyers and sellers. Rapid turnover of large quantities of goods is achieved at narrow margins of profit.

Japan's ability to perform feats of export expansion owes much to trading company activities. Each trading company markets hundreds of products and can efficiently fill its large ships with many small orders. For a small producer whose export sales are below the minimum volume that would make an export effort economic, the trading company offers an efficient and inexpensive way of arranging transport, establishing inventory, and reaching customers. The result is worldwide export market access for smaller Japanese companies for products whose export market potential is still limited and to countries whose market is small.

The lack of a comparable marketing institution in the United States hampers the potential exports of smaller American companies that cannot economically justify the effort and cost involved, particularly to markets of limited size. In some cases, the chief executive of a U.S. company simply does not have the will to tackle exports when faced with the countervailing attractions of the U.S. market. A Japanese-style trading company with offices all over the world would reduce the cost of exporting and would make fewer demands on the attention of the chief executive.

IMPORT RESTRICTIONS AND EXPORT INCENTIVES

Japan's attitudes toward trade have been conditioned by a century of effort to reach industrial parity and a century of experience with a fragile balance of payments. Until very recently, Japan has tended to view exports as a means of paying for raw materials and for debt service rather than as a means of obtaining goods for consumption at lower cost. Traditional Japanese foreign trade policy has therefore aimed at maximizing exports and minimizing imports through a large and complex network of import restrictions and export inducements.

Tariffs. Tariffs and import quotas constitute the traditional instruments of import restriction. As a consequence of a series of multilateral negotiations culminating in the Kennedy Round, however, the role of tariffs has been substantially reduced.

Before the first phase of Kennedy Round tariff cuts was put into effect in 1968, Japanese tariffs on dutiable imports were 15 to 20 percent. When the final Kennedy Round reductions were put into effect in 1971, the average tariff rate on dutiable imports was reduced to about 11 percent. Although this average is only slightly higher than that of the United States or the European Community, tariffs on finished consumer goods remain relatively high. Moreover, as in all countries where tariffs are lower on raw materials than on successive stages of processing, the "effective protection" on the manufacturing process is greater than the nominal tariff on the final product.*

Thus, although tariffs have declined in relative importance, they still represent substantial trade barriers in certain product categories. Among the aims of the new multilateral trade negotiations is the progressive reduction of tariffs by industrial countries.

Import Quotas. In the immediate postwar period, Japan, like Europe, was compelled to impose strict controls over trade and capital flows to conserve scarce foreign exchange. Throughout the fifties, these controls were regarded as a necessary means of stimulating domestic production and safeguarding the balance of payments. Indeed, until 1963, Japan's quantitative restrictions on imports were justified under the balance-of-payments exception of GATT. But Japan has maintained import quotas long after such restrictions could be justified on balance-of-payments grounds.

At the time of Japan's accession to the IMF in 1963, over 200 items were under restriction. From 1963 to 1965, a large number of items were liberalized; many of them, however, were noncompeting raw materials. From 1965 to 1969, Japanese restrictions remained intact despite Japan's transition to a payments surplus position. To some extent, the Kennedy Round and its aftermath diverted attention during this period from quantitative restrictions to tariffs. But since 1970, Japan has accelerated its

---

* If an article costing $1.00 has in it $.50 worth of raw materials that are duty-free, then a 10 percent nominal tariff on the finished product provides 20 percent effective protection for the manufacturing process.

liberalization of import quotas in response to strong pressures from other countries. By April 1973, Japan had reduced the number of items under quota to 32, of which 24 were agricultural and marine products and 8 were mining and industrial products, including coal, leather goods, computers and accessories, and integrated circuits. At both ends of this spectrum (agricultural and high-technology products), items are included that frustrate the obvious comparative advantage of the United States.

The restrictions on imports of agricultural and mining products are defended on social policy grounds; whereas those on computers and integrated circuits are defended as infant-industry protection in line with the nation's industrial policy. Some estimates of the potential contribution of complete quota removal on Japan's trade balance show only modest results. Nevertheless, those remaining restrictions that are inconsistent with GATT should be promptly eliminated.

Other Trade Barriers. In addition to import quotas and tariffs, a major obstacle to the sale of U.S. products in Japan is posed by the archaic internal distribution system and by restrictions on foreign investment in retail operations. Japan also has a multiplicity of informal controls on imports, such as administrative guidance, preferences on government purchasing, and customs practices. With the large tariff cuts under the Kennedy Round and the progressive removal of import quotas, other types of barriers have become matters of greater concern and prominent targets for foreign criticism. There is an urgent need to cope with these obstacles in order to achieve the full benefits of past trade liberalization and to prevent the erosion of these benefits.

Informal barriers vary considerably in their importance. Many are of only marginal significance, but some have substantial effects on competition and hence on the volume and pattern of international trade. One type of control, the system of administrative guidance, deserves special comment. Administrative guidance is the informal pressure that the government exerts on Japanese business. It is effective because of the high degree of dependence of the private sector on various forms of government support. Numerous joint government-business associations are the transmission lines through which guidance is passed to prospective importers. Although Japan has not been alone in using administrative controls to inhibit imports, it is unique in the extent to which the system has been used as an important tool of economic policy.

It would be a mistake, however, to assume that an army of government bureaucrats check all pending import applications with a view to maximizing their diversion to domestic suppliers. The system is not that well organized, nor are there enough bureaucrats to control all the different types of transactions. By and large, the system is brought into play for major transactions. Nevertheless, it is clearly a restraint on trade.

Another measure that has a trade-deterrent effect and has caused considerable concern among American producers is the Japanese internal commodity tax, under which differential rates are applied on automobiles, depending on engine capacity, wheel base, and body width. Although the differential was recently reduced, standard-size U.S. cars are subject to a 20 percent rate (40 percent before April 1973) as compared with 15 percent for almost all Japanese cars. Although the tax may appear discriminatory, it is justified as a means of penalizing those who consume larger quantities of limited energy resources and who contribute most to pollution.

The problem of pollution illustrates the broader question of how to cope with the international competitive distortions that could result from perfectly legitimate efforts of individual countries to achieve their own social and economic goals. Both the United States and Japan have agreed in the OECD to observe the polluter-pays principle in financing the costs of pollution control measures. The OECD guidelines also call on governments to adopt more stringent standards of environmental protection and to seek the harmonization of environmental policies where valid reasons for differences do not exist. In short, governments are called upon to frame their environmental policy so as to avoid the creation of new nontariff barriers to trade.

A major international effort will be undertaken in the forthcoming multilateral trade negotiations to deal with the problem of nontariff distortions of trade. Some guidelines are offered in the joint policy statement *Nontariff Distortions of Trade* issued in 1969 by CED, Keizai Doyukai, and other counterpart organizations.

Export Incentives. Business, banking, and government have worked together in Japan to see that export targets are fulfilled, and measures to promote exports have been an integral part of Japanese industrial strategy. In the past, export incentives have included: liberal depreciation allowances for exports; tax exemption on income from exports (terminated in 1964); liberal write-offs for export development expenses; preferential credit rationing and lower discount rates on export bills; and a comprehensive government export insurance system. Today, almost all these measures have been repealed. The liberal depreciation allowances and tax write-offs were suspended or repealed in 1971. The Bank of Japan's lower discount rates on export bills were raised, and preferential treatment of export financing was virtually terminated by the end of 1972.

Progress made by Japan during the early seventies in eliminating import quotas and export incentives represented a significant change in its traditional policy. But the long delay and the piecemeal procedure substantially diluted the psychological impact of the liberalization. It is hoped that the current turnaround in the Japanese payments position will not lead to a reversal of the course of liberalization that Japan has been pursuing.

On the other hand, if Japanese import liberalization has been a slow process, it is also true that Japanese exports are severely restricted by almost all European countries and to a much lesser extent by the United States. So long as Western Europe lags well behind the United States in its willingness to accept Japanese products, the U.S. market will continue to be the major target for Japanese exporters. In steel, for example, the much-tighter European restrictions have caused a deflection of Japanese exports to the United States. Furthermore, the Japanese government will be tempted to slow the pace of its own liberalization efforts if European discrimination continues on its present scale. The United States and Japan share an interest in pressing the European governments to accelerate the pace at which they remove present restrictions on Japanese imports.

IMPACT OF INDUSTRIAL POLICY
ON TRADE

The government's industrial policy has played an important role in making Japan a formidable competitor in world markets. The government selected priority industries with promising export possibilities and promoted them through various means, including preferential credit rationing, tax exemptions, extremely liberal depreciation allowances, and encouragement of imports of Western technology. In addition, industrial policy has comprehended the reduction of foreign competition and the promotion of import substitution through various forms of protection for weaker producers or infant industries.

Although domestic measures designed to strengthen or adjust industrial structures are not always well coordinated, they are nevertheless rather common in industrial countries. To the extent that these measures are intended to increase efficiency, improve the quality of products, and reduce costs, they do not conflict with the interests of other countries. But there are some industrial policy measures, however respectable their objectives may be, that nevertheless distort trade and undermine an optimal international division of labor.

Governments, of course, cannot follow a policy of complete nonintervention in the activities of domestic industries solely in the interest of international trade. However, the industrial countries now have so great an exposure to one another that what any one of them does about its own industrial policy tends to influence and be influenced by the actions of others. Therefore, it is important that when formulating their domestic policies they seek to make them compatible with a liberal system of international trade. Measures taken must not be used as a means of granting disguised protection or giving domestic producers an advantage in foreign markets. Furthermore, in pursuing domestic aims, governments should endeavor to use measures that have the fewest harmful consequences for their trade partners and create the least possible distortion in international competition.

VOLUNTARY EXPORT RESTRAINTS AND ORDERLY MARKETING

Japan has been the major target of U.S. attempts to get other countries to impose "voluntary" export quotas. The use of voluntary export restraints, often worked out bilaterally under the threat of mandatory import quotas, represents a growing problem. The arrangements are often not publicized so that their scope is not fully known. Yet trade flows are affected by this network of barriers, and the matter is one of concern to the whole trading community.

Voluntary export restraints are also imposed on the initiative of the Japanese themselves to prevent excessive competition among their own exporters. When it is desired to avoid the pressure on prices resulting from cutthroat selling competition, voluntary export restraints are applied in order to realize "orderly marketing" even in the absence of a threat of import restrictions by foreign countries. Restraints of this type outnumber those requested by importing countries. It is estimated that the total number of items currently subject to either type of export restraint exceeds 200.

Export controls in Japan are usually carried out either through export cartels formed under the Export-Import Transaction Law (1952) or through the Export Trade Control Ordinance, a cabinet order enacted in accordance with the provisions of the Foreign Exchange and Foreign Trade Control Law (1949). These statutes were originally designed to promote export expansion but are now used more often to impose restraints on exports.

The Export-Import Transaction Law provides for the formation of voluntary export cartels. Its original objectives were to reduce excessive competition among Japanese exporters and to encourage their cooperation in long-run development of export markets. For this purpose, exporters were exempted from the provisions of the antitrust laws. In the 1970s, however, export cartels are being used as a means of enforcing orderly marketing. They often receive administrative guidance from MITI concerning export levels and the distribution of export quotas among the cartel's members. This form of orderly marketing is the most typical form of export restraint.

Under the Export Trade Control Ordinance, on the other hand, orderly marketing is not voluntary. The restraints are entirely and explicitly enforced by the government. Most of the bilateral voluntary export control agreements concluded between the United States and Japan are enforced under the ordinance. This type of control has always been strongly resisted by Japanese exporters, and it has been regarded by MITI as a last resort.

Although the concept of orderly marketing covers a wide range, it is evident that the United States and Japan have interpreted it in different ways. From the American point of view, it means that Japan will exercise control over exports and adhere to export quotas. From the Japanese point of view, however, the concept is broader. It means the setting of "reasonable" export prices, the establishment of export cartels, the diversification of export markets, and the development of new export commodities. The policy therefore connotes the orderly development of export trade in order to avoid unnecessary frictions in importing countries while accommodating the desired structural change in the economy. Because of the difference in their respective notions of what export restraint means, its results are likewise subject to different interpretations by the United States and Japan. Moreover, the quotas are for the most part not public information; consequently, the restraints cannot be quantitatively evaluated.

There are good reasons for misgivings concerning this type of export restraint. It offends the basic principles of a liberal trading regime and raises sensitive questions about the antitrust laws of both Japan and its trade partners. The restraints imposed in response to U.S. pressure are equivalent to U.S. import quotas, yet they are imposed without benefit of the open hearings and other procedures required under U.S. law. They serve as a strong inducement to the formation of cartels in Japan as a means of administering the quotas.

The export restraints that Japan has been required to impose or that have been imposed voluntarily should have an important place in the pending trade negotiations. In their evasion of formal discrimination, the controls remain the major mark of Japan's less than full membership in the trading system of the industrialized nations. Japan has accepted export restraints in the belief that they have prevented American imposition of import restrictions that might have been more stringent or have affected a greater range of products. In some circumstances, export controls can be more flexible than import restrictions and may be easier to remove when circumstances change, but present trends do not warrant too optimistic a view. The European practice of formalizing export quotas in bilateral agreements invites acceptance of the idea that export quotas should be regarded as normal forms of trade restriction, a view that might well encourage their wider use. The forthcoming trade negotiations will provide an appropriate occasion to work toward phasing out Japanese export quotas.

DUMPING AND UNFAIR COMPETITION

The charges of Japanese dumping and unfair competition have been one of the troublesome aspects of U.S.-Japanese trade relations. Dumping, defined as the practice of selling goods for export at a lower price than in the home market, is condemned by GATT if it causes material injury to competing producers in the importing country. The U.S. Antidumping Act provides for special duties to offset the "margin of dumping" if injury is found.

Since the Antidumping Act became U.S. law in 1921, well over one hundred complaints have been brought against Japanese exports. Prior to 1970, however, only four cases were found to be injurious to domestic firms. More recently, the U.S. Tariff Commission has found injury to domestic firms in several cases. Although the dumping that has recently ocurred has involved differential pricing, it has not been predatory dumping, a practice designed to capture a foreign market by selling below cost until the competition is driven out.

A special type of export drive practiced by Japanese firms may help to account for frequent complaints about unfair competition. With the high fixed obligations of a lifetime employment system and heavy debt, Japanese corporations look abroad for cash especially when domestic demand is sluggish. This situation has been referred to as supply-oriented exports and has tended to exert pressure on Japanese firms to push their products into exports so long as variable costs can be recovered. In fact, much of Japan's export growth appears to have been based on the domestic economy supporting the fixed costs and export markets covering little more than variable costs.

Future developments in Japan may make this problem less acute. As the rate of growth of domestic markets for a product slows, its capacity to absorb fixed costs also diminishes, so that the ability to expand exports at lower costs is reduced. Moreover, in the past, Japanese customers accepted goods at whatever price they were offered. Recently, however, they have begun to take a more critical view of the so-called recession cartels that have enabled Japanese manufacturers to price goods higher in the domestic market than abroad. A consumer boycott in 1970 forced Japanese television manufacturers to align their domestic prices with the prices charged in foreign markets. To the extent that Japanese consumer interests become more active in the future, the Japanese dumping problem may be alleviated. As noted earlier, dumping and discriminatory pricing in the U.S. market is likely to run afoul of U.S. laws and into the danger of severe penalties.

Because of the archaic and fragmented nature of the internal Japanese distribution system, a price discrepancy between domestic and foreign sales at the retail level need not necessarily reflect dumping. With the same factory price for domestic sale and for export, the chances are that a product will be sold at a lower price through a mail-order catalogue in the United States than in the typical small retail outlet in Japan.

On the other hand, the operations of Japanese trading companies, particularly the sole importer system, tend to generate a prima facie case of dumping in cases of currency realignments. Instead of lowering the domestic price of imported goods when the yen is revalued, the Japanese importer commonly increases his profit. At the same time, the excess profits on imports are used to reduce the price of exports, thereby offsetting the effect of the revaluation on the export side. This practice constitutes a major nontariff distortion of trade and should be phased out.

STRUCTURE OF JAPANESE TRADE AND ITS IMPLICATIONS

Three features of Japan's trade were closely associated with the difficulties it had with its major trading partners: (1) the strikingly low ratio of imports of manufactures, particularly of manufactured consumer goods; (2) the high degree of dependence on exports in a number of key industries; and (3) the concentration of export markets in a small number of countries.

Japan still remains a limited market for imported manufactures. In this respect, it lags behind not only the major Western European countries but even a number of smaller industrial countries. An earlier revaluation of the yen and a more liberal import policy might well have avoided the type of built-in rigidity in import structure that led to the difficulties Japan experienced in its effort to increase imports and hence reduce its balance-of-payments surpluses.

The role of foreign trade in the Japanese economy is usually underestimated because the aggregate ratio of exports to GNP (9.8 percent in 1970) conceals the dependence of key industries on exports. Although the share of exports in total production has remained relatively stable, the export-to-output ratio has been rising rapidly in a number of key industries. In some of these industries, the export ratios have reached levels seldom encountered in even the most export-intensive economies of Western Europe. In the iron and steel industry, for example, exports amounted to more than one-quarter of total production in 1970. The export ratio exceeded one-quarter of total production in motor vehicles, consumer electronics, ships, petrochemical products, fertilizers, and textiles. Given this dependence, the pressure to export is very high, particularly in times of slack in domestic demand, when it has often led to the charge of market disruption.

Although Japan's share in world exports increased in virtually all markets during the 1960s, the export effort was heavily concentrated on the United States and the rapidly expanding smaller Asian economies (Korea, Taiwan, Hong Kong, and Singapore). In the United States, the proportion of total imports of manufactures supplied by Japan rose from about 7 percent in 1955 to more than 20 percent in 1970. The competition from Japanese imports has become particularly intensive in steel, automobiles, synthetic textiles, and television sets, and it has been a major contributor to a rise in the protectionist mood. Japan's share in the imports of Asian countries also rose significantly, from about 10 percent in 1955 to 26 percent in 1970. At the same time, Japan's failure to increase its imports of manufactured goods has become a source of complaint among the Asian countries.

FUTURE DEVELOPMENT OF JAPANESE TRADE

A number of factors should tend to diminish present Japanese competitiveness. First, the recent revaluations and floating of the yen have made Japanese goods more expensive in foreign markets. Second, a growing assertiveness on the part of Japanese labor unions in relation to wages and fringe benefits may increase production costs more rapidly in the future. Third, an intensification of labor shortages and a deceleration in the shift in employment from agriculture to industry and services will speed the rise in labor costs. These trends in production costs in Japan have been one of the main factors leading many Japanese firms in labor-intensive industries to site their foreign operations in the low-wage countries of Southeast Asia. Fourth, the costs of acquiring the latest technology in today's growth industries will rise as the Japanese find it necessary to develop their own technology rather than buy it cheaply from abroad as in the past. A more normal rate of growth in basic primary industries, such as metals and chemicals, will reduce the opportunity for applying new technology. Fifth, increasing government expenditures on housing, infrastructure, pollution control, and social services will tend to divert resources from investment in tradable goods. Finally, rising energy and raw material costs will increase the price of Japanese goods abroad.

In the coming decade, Japanese imports are likely to increase more rapidly than in the past. First, the fall in the yen prices of many foreign products relative to domestic goods as a result of the yen revaluation will accelerate the growth of imports. Second, rising relative prices of energy and some raw materials will step up Japan's import bill. Third, the propensity to import is likely to rise as personal income rises and consumer demand for manufactured goods increases. Fourth, the worldwide tendency of raw-material-exporting nations to require local processing is bound to augment the cost of Japan's imports, particularly of petrochemicals. Finally, preferential Japanese tariffs on imports from developing countries will augment the tendency already apparent to rely increasingly on imports for labor-intensive products.

4. Foreign Investment

••••••••••••••••••••••••••••••

JAPAN'S POSTWAR POLICY toward foreign investment has undergone a major transformation from an inward and restrictive policy, which was followed until the latter part of the 1960s, to a policy that is now contributing in a major way to the internationalization of the Japanese economy. As host to the international corporation, Japan has come a long way in recent years in liberalizing the terms on which direct foreign investment can acquire assets and conduct their operations. And Japanese firms have themselves emerged as major investors abroad, stimulated especially by the desire to control sources of scarce raw materials and to free themselves from domestic environmental constraints and labor shortages.

FOREIGN INVESTMENT IN JAPAN

Foreign capital has played only a negligible role in Japanese economic growth because Japan has historically sought to insulate its economy from any semblance of external domination or control. Even when Japan was in great need of additional resources for investment, restric-

52

tions were maintained on the entry of foreign capital, particularly in the form of direct investment. Until the early part of the 1960s, the flow of foreign direct investment into Japan had been insignificant, perhaps not so much as a result of Japan's restrictive policy but rather because Japan had not yet become recognized as an appealing market for foreign investors. As the attractiveness of the market grew, foreign enterprises began to show keen interest in investing but found themselves severely restricted by Japanese government policy.

Apart from the fear of foreign domination, Japan's resistance to foreign investment is related to the active role of the government in promoting industrialization ever since the latter part of the nineteenth century. In directing the growth process, the government has preferred to work with Japanese rather than foreign businessmen since, in its view, the latter could not be relied on to accept administrative guidance and to participate in other ways in the delicate business-government relationship characteristic of Japanese economic life. In addition, there has been a deep-seated anxiety that foreign firms would disrupt industrial order by ill-timed wage increases or by otherwise deviating from traditional practices in such activities as hiring and promoting. These factors have reinforced the high degree of group solidarity and ethnocentrism underlying Japan's traditional resistance to the intrusion of foreign investment.

Volume and Structure of Capital Inflow. Until the late 1960s, the bulk of long-term capital inflow into Japan was in the form of loans. Direct investment and portfolio investment in the form of acquisition of stocks without participation in management accounted for less than one-third of the capital inflow. The pattern began to change in 1968 when the inflow of capital in the form of stock purchases accelerated, reaching an annual average of $2 billion in the period from 1969 to 1971. In 1972, this form of capital inflow doubled to almost $4 billion. The sudden increase appears, however, to have been stimulated by the anticipation of the second yen revaluation that took place in February 1973.

The annual flow of foreign direct investment remained at less than $100 million until 1970. It has been only in recent years that the annual flow has reached $200 million. As of March 1973, the accumulated total of direct investments amounted to about $900 million; whereas stock purchases totaled $13.2 billion, and loans totaled $8.8 billion (see Table 6).

Foreign direct investment in Japan is concentrated in three industries: petroleum, chemicals, and machinery. Most of the enterprises are joint ventures that were originally established as a means of either obtaining essential raw materials or acquiring foreign technology not obtainable through straight licensing arrangements. Although Japan is the world's largest importer of crude oil, it had no alternative until recently but to rely on the major international oil companies as sources of supply. As a consequence, petroleum is the one field in which foreign investment dominates. In the cases of chemicals and machinery, joint enterprises proved to be the only means whereby Japan could obtain the technology it wanted.

As of March 1971, the United States accounted for more than two-thirds of foreign direct investment in Japan. This dominance is due to the earlier interest of American companies in the Japanese market, the close trading relations between the two countries, and the fact that the United States has been the major source of foreign technology.

Recent Evolution of Foreign Investment Policy. Japan has only slowly and reluctantly relaxed its restrictive policy toward foreign capital. When Japan joined the OECD in 1964, it adopted in principle the OECD code of capital liberalization, but it was not until 1967 that the first modest steps were taken to relax the rules on foreign direct investment. This action was followed by several others, culminating in the fifth round of liberalization effective beginning in May 1973. The new measures, applicable both to newly established ventures and to existing enterprises, permit full ownership by foreign investors, except for a small number of specifically designated industries. Before this round of liberalization, the governing principle was to limit foreign ownership to 50 percent in most of the important industries.

During the previous four rounds of liberalization, Japan had liberalized 228 categories of industries for 100 percent foreign ownership while keeping about 700 industries under a 50 percent ownership rule. Only with its latest round of liberalization did Japan show its willingness to grant a degree of freedom for foreign investors comparable with that accorded in most other industrial countries. Considering the highly restrictive inward investment policy of the preceding two decades, Japan has made a great deal of progress during the past several years.

Japan's capital liberalization, an essential element in the internationalization of the country's economy, has been strongly influenced by external forces, particularly by persistent pressure from the United States. After the fourth round of liberalization, criticism of Japan's policy centered on two features: the continued adherence to the 50 percent limitation of foreign ownership in new ventures and the stringent restrictions on the acquisition of shares in existing enterprises.

Table 6. JAPAN'S LONG-TERM INVESTMENT POSITION, SELECTED YEARS
(millions of dollars)

Fiscal Years	INFLOW				OUTFLOW		
	Direct Investment	Portfolio Investment	Bank Loans	Total Inflow	Direct[a] Investment	Bank Loans	Total Outflow
1951–1955 average	5	3	30	38	} 19	} 10	} 29
1956–1960 average	13	22	141	176			
1961–1965 average	36	224	456	716	93	40	133
1966–1970 average	56	1,085	710	1,851	217	311	528
1966	40	87	330	457	105	122	227
1967	30	180	638	848	140	135	275
1968	53	837	947	1,837	229	328	557
1969	54	2,644	790	3,488	261	404	665
1970	91	1,687	846	2,624	334	570	904
1971	224	2,578	971	3,773	525	333	858
1972	136	3,969	1,137	5,242	2,086	252	2,338
Cumulative total, 1951–1972	899	13,230	8,792	22,921	4,332	2,441	6,773

Note: The data are on approval bases, which differ from balance-of-payments data. The approval data show only "gross flows," and do not take account of either repayments of foreign capital or repatriation of invested capital.
[a]Includes negligible amount of portfolio investments.

Source: Bank of Japan, Manual of Foreign Investment in Japan (November 1971); Kikan Gaikoku-Gawase [Quarterly Journal of Foreign Exchange] (January–March 1973); MITI, Trade Promotion Bureau, Economic Cooperation and Its Problems (1971); and Tsusanshō Gōhō [MITI Bulletin], August 7, 1973.

Following are the main elements of the fifth round of liberalization.

1. *Establishment of new firms.* Full ownership by foreign investors (100 percent liberalization) is allowed except for twenty-two industries. Of these, seventeen will be opened to 100 percent foreign ownership within two or three years, and five will remain in the restricted catagory.

The five sectors in which foreign investments continue to be restricted are agriculture, forestry, and fisheries (treated as a single line of industry); mining; oil refining; leather and leather goods manufacturing; and retail trade. In these industries, foreign investments are subject to individual screening by the relevant ministries (the Ministry of Finance and the ministry with jurisdiction over the industry concerned). In mining, however, an automatic approval system is to prevail if the foreign ownership does not exceed 50 percent. Investments in retail trade are also subject to automatic approval if the foreign participation does not exceed 50 percent and if the total number of stores in each retail chain does not exceed eleven. (This retail trade concession was obtained at the 1972 Hakone meeting of American and Japanese trade officials.)

The seventeen industries where complete liberalization is delayed until fixed target dates are mostly food processing, some chemical and metal industries, and high-technology industries such as computer manufacturing. In the case of the computer and computer-related industries, liberalization was to take place in two stages: 50 percent ownership in the first stage beginning August 1974, and full ownership within the three-year limit. It is understood, however, that some delay is now contemplated in liberalization of the computer industry.

2. *Acquisition of stocks of existing enterprises.* Another sweeping change in the fifth round of liberalization was the removal of the stringent restrictions on the acquisition of stock of existing enterprises. Foreign investors are now allowed to acquire up to 100 percent of the equity of existing Japanese enterprises on the condition that the consent of the enterprise is obtained. Where there is no such consent, past regulations would presumably apply; that is, foreign participation would be limited to a maximum of 10 percent for any single investor and 25 percent for all foreign investors. Although the consent requirement needs to be tested, Japan seems to be moving toward the principle of full foreign ownership in both new and existing enterprises.

Impetus for Full Liberalization. The principal opposition to full capital liberalization has come from small business, which still occupies an important place in the Japanese economy. At the same time, the change in attitude among the leaders of Japan's most dynamic business sectors has provided the main impetus for liberalization.

Japanese business leaders had become increasingly concerned over the passive attitude of the government, which they felt had given an impression to the rest of the world that Japan was reneging on its international obligations. Sensing the inevitability of capital liberalization, they believed it would be in Japan's long-run national interest to seize the initiative rather than to react reluctantly to external pressures. They also see capital liberalization as a bargaining instrument to improve the climate for Japanese exports. In addition, they believe that eventually Japanese corporations too must become multinational in order to remain viable in the international market. Japanese direct foreign investment abroad is still modest, but it is increasing at a rapid rate. It is obvious that Japan must relax its own restrictions before it can demand more favorable treatment for Japanese investment overseas.

Particularly onerous are the remaining Japanese restrictions on foreign investment in retail distribution. Japanese firms are free to open new stores and servicing facilities in the United States without limit, yet Japan restricts U.S. retail outlets to not more than eleven per applicant. These restrictions amount in effect to obstacles to trade since many American products cannot compete in the Japanese market if they must bear the cumulative markups of the multilayered and fragmented Japanese distribution system. Liberalization of foreign investment is in the long-run interest of Japan and is an essential element in moving toward an open world economy.

JAPANESE INVESTMENT ABROAD

Volume and Structure. Japan's overseas investment has been expanding rapidly in recent years. In the early postwar years, Japanese corporations had neither the desire nor the financial resources to invest abroad. The annual flow of Japanese investment remained at less than $200 million until the middle of the 1960s, but rose to $900 million in 1970 and to $2.3 billion in 1972 (see Table 6). Most of the increase in 1972 consisted of a rapid step-up in direct investment, from $525 million in 1971 to $2.08 billion in 1972. This record increase in 1972 was stimulated by Japan's sharply rising foreign exchange reserves. As of March 1973, outstanding foreign investment of Japan totaled $6.8 billion, of which $4.3 billion was direct investment and $2.4 billion was in the form of loans.

By international standards, however, Japanese foreign investment as a percent of GNP is still rather low. Japan's outstanding direct investments abroad were equivalent to 2.3 percent of its GNP in 1972, as compared to 8.2 percent for the United States and about 4 percent for West Germany. In 1970, output of Japan's foreign subsidiaries was equal to only a little over 30 percent of Japan's annual exports, whereas the production of U.S. foreign subsidiaries was almost four times as much as U.S. exports.

Japan's overseas investments are heavily concentrated in resource development as a means of ensuring greater stability of supplies for its industry. In addition, Japanese foreign investment is motivated by the desire to expand markets for exports and to take advantage of low-cost labor and land as well as foreign environmental resources. The bulk of investments in commerce, banking, and insurance are in North America and Western Europe, whereas manufacturing investments have tended to concentrate in Southeast Asia. Overall, the geographical distribution of Japanese foreign investment closely parallels the pattern of its export markets. About one-fourth of Japanese investments are in North America, followed by Southeast Asia, which accounts for 23 percent. A relatively large portion of total investment (16 percent) has gone to Latin America because its natural resources have presented attractive opportunities. In the aggregate, about 50 percent of Japan's overseas investment has gone to developing countries, where it constitutes an important element of Japan's economic relations with these countries. This pattern differs from that of other industrial countries, which invest largely in each other.

Another unique feature of Japanese foreign investment is the large involvement of Japanese trading companies. About one out of every four foreign ventures is undertaken by the ten top general trading firms, with Mitsui and Mitsubishi the leaders.

Regulations. Japanese investment abroad is regulated under the foreign exchange control law of 1949 and subsequent legislation and administrative rulings. It was only in June 1971 that Japan removed most of its restrictions on overseas investments. Prior to June 1971, every case of foreign investment and each increase of capital had to be individually approved by the Ministry of Finance, which usually consulted with other appropriate ministries, especially MITI. This system of individual screening was changed into one of automatic approval by the Bank of Japan in 1971. The application, however, must provide a great deal of information about the project and its background. There are no published requirements for approval, but it is generally understood that the following are among the principal criteria for an investment: it must promote exports from Japan or develop natural resources unavailable or scarce in Japan; it must not undermine the effectiveness of domestic monetary policy; and it must not contribute to "excessive" competition, a euphemism for hurting other Japanese firms at home.

The sharp turnaround in Japan's balance of payments in 1973 has compelled the government to take another hard look at its overseas investment policy. The result is likely to be a realignment of investment activities. Although foreign direct investment in raw materials or for industrial development is likely to continue to be encouraged, ventures of a speculative type (e.g., real estate) are likely to be curtailed.

Prospects. The currency realignments since 1971 may well lead to a convergence in the degree of multinationalization of business enterprise of the United States and Japan. In prior years, one of the attractions for American firms to invest in productive facilities abroad was the overvaluation of the dollar, which made foreign assets and factor costs cheap. In the case of Japan, on the other hand, there was little incentive with an undervalued yen to establish manufacturing facilities abroad. The recent corrections of these major exchange rate distortions should exert some tendency toward moderating the pace of U.S. investment abroad while accelerating the multinationalization of Japanese firms.

How fast Japanese foreign investment will increase is difficult to predict. According to a forecast by MITI before the oil crisis, total investment will rise from $4 billion in 1972 to $26 billion in 1980. Whatever the precise level, a rapid increase in Japanese foreign investment is bound to take place. Foreign investment is one of the important means by which Japanese firms are attempting to ensure a steady flow of raw materials at reasonable prices. The growing shortage of labor and rising wages in Japan will increasingly force Japanese firms in labor-intensive industries to move their production to lower-wage areas abroad. Japan's preferential tariffs on manufactures from developing countries may also contribute to accelerating this trend. The steeply rising cost of land may induce some land-intensive industries to go abroad in search of cheaper locations.

A closely related factor concerns the cost of pollution. Japan is so densely developed, with the highest GNP per usable acre in the world, that pollution has become a critical problem. It has already become difficult for some industries to find suitable sites in Japan without meeting public resistance against possible environmental disruptions. The cost of controlling pollution is becoming increasingly expensive as the government begins to enforce more stringent antipollution regulations. Recently, some of Japan's chemical companies have had to meet demands for compensation from fishermen whose catches were found to contain unacceptable levels of heavy metals and other long-lasting pollutants. Some Japanese industries that are heavy polluters are already finding it more profitable to produce abroad in countries where nature can still handle more wastes or where the government is less concerned over the consequences of pollution. Some Japanese mineral producers have already begun to smelt ores in other countries for this reason.

Japanese as well as American firms are facing a set of unique challenges, namely, how to set up workable arrangements for investment in the Soviet Union. The Asiatic regions of the Soviet Union contain substantial deposits of valuable but undeveloped natural resources including oil and gas. Foreign technology, capital, and markets could contribute immeasurably to the profitable exploitation of these Soviet resources. Some progress has already been made in working out arrangements with the Soviet Union. The proposed arrangements are somewhat similar to those under which Japan has participated in the development of Australia's resources. Collaboration between American and Japanese firms in these endeavors is a subject worthy of further exploration.

Problems. Foreign investment always stirs opposition because some local firms suffer under the added competition. Nationalistic feeling is particularly agitated by foreign investment in natural resources, especially nonreplaceable resources such as petroleum and minerals, in which the Japanese have shown a special interest. Southeast Asia is a particularly sensitive area where increasing opposition is developing against alleged economic domination by Japan. These problems will pose a major challenge to Japanese firms, which will have to learn how to survive in a somewhat hostile environment.

In this respect, Japanese firms have already shown a high degree of flexibility. They have often accommodated to nationalistic sentiment in host countries by providing capital on a long-term loan basis as well as in the form of direct investments. They have also been quite ready to experiment with such other techniques as production-sharing arrangements, management contracts, and technology transfers independent of equity and management participation. Moreover, Japanese overseas investment has shown, at least until recently, a strong representation of smaller-scale enterprises with technology more appropriate to the resource endowments of the developing countries.

5. Raw Materials

· ·

I<small>T IS WELL KNOWN</small> that Japan is poor in natural resources and depends heavily on imports to meet its raw material needs. The availability as well as costs of raw materials on international markets are much more important to the Japanese economy than to any other industrial country. In spite of years of effort to ensure access to foreign sources of resources, however, the vulnerability of Japan as a resource-poor country has been clearly shown by recent developments in the world oil market.

TRENDS IN THE DEMAND AND SUPPLY OF MATERIALS

Japanese consumption of resources has increased to account for a large proportion of the world's total requirements just at a time when the international supply, particularly of energy resources, has become subject to major uncertainties. Japan is today the second largest consumer of raw materials in the noncommunist world and the world's largest importer.

It depends heavily on imported supplies of minerals, including petroleum, iron ore, coking coal, bauxite, nickel, tin, lead, zinc, copper, and manganese. Japan also imports a number of nonmineral materials in large

61

Table 7. AVERAGE ANNUAL RATE OF INCREASE IN THE CONSUMPTION OF MINERALS, SELECTED COUNTRIES, 1964–1969 (percent)

	Petro-leum	Crude steel	Alumi-num	Copper	Lead	Zinc	Nickel	Average annual rate of increase in real GNP
Japan	17.4	14.5	22.5	12.0	3.2	9.5	17.5	10.9
United States	5.0	3.3	7.5	3.0	5.0	2.5	—	4.6
France	11.1	5.3	8.0	2.5	2.9	3.3	9.2	5.5
West Germany	11.6	3.9	10.8	3.4	5.0	—	7.4	4.7
Italy	9.7	11.6	13.8	3.7	11.8	6.4	13.8	5.4
United Kingdom	7.6	0.8	2.0	—	—	—	—	2.3
Total, free world countries	8.1	—	9.5	3.2	3.8	3.0	4.3	—

Source: MITI, *Shigen Mondai no Tenbo* [White Paper on Natural Resources] (1971).

quantity, such as lumber, cotton, rubber, and wool. Together these products accounted for more than half of Japan's total imports in 1972. As shown in Table 7, the rate of increase in Japan's consumption of mineral resources (except for lead) exceeded that of any other industrial country.

By 1971, Japan accounted for 10.8 percent of the free world's total consumption of petroleum. For other minerals such as aluminum and copper, Japan's share was even larger, accounting for 11.3 and 14.6 percent, respectively, of the free world's total consumption.

Per unit of GNP, Japan's consumption of mineral resources was the highest among major industrial countries. The combined value of seven major minerals (petroleum, crude steel, copper, lead, zinc, nickel, and

62

Table 8. IMPORTS AS A PERCENT
OF JAPAN'S TOTAL CONSUMPTION OF
SELECTED RAW MATERIALS, 1960–1975

	1960	1970	1975 (projection)
Copper	51	76	82
Lead	55	55	46
Zinc	26	55	57
Aluminum	100	100	100
Nickel	100	100	100
Iron ore	68	88	91
Coking coal	36	76	83
Petroleum	99	100	100
Natural gas	0	35	74
Uranium	—	100	100
Weighted average of the ten resources	71	90	93

Source: MITI, Shigen Mondai no Tenbo [White Paper on Natural Resources] (1971).

aluminum) consumed to produce $1,000 of GNP in 1969 was $76 for Japan, as compared with $60 for West Germany and $41 for the United States. The high figure for Japan reflects the greater role of heavy industries in its economy.

Along with a rapid increase in consumption, Japan's dependence on foreign mineral resources rose significantly over the decade of the sixties. The weighted average of the ratio of imports to consumption for ten major minerals increased from 71 percent in 1960 to 90 percent in 1970 (see Table 8). On an individual product basis, the import-dependence ratio in 1970 was 100 percent for aluminum, nickel, and uranium; 99.7 percent for petroleum; and 88 percent for iron ore. The comparable ratios for other minerals ranged from 35 percent for natural gas to 78 percent for coking coal. The increasing dependence on imported minerals resulted in a rising share of these products in the country's total imports, from 38.7 percent in 1960 to 44.3 percent in 1970.

Until the late 1960s, Japan had experienced little difficulty in purchasing on the open market the raw materials needed from aboard. Most materials were in oversupply, so that prices and other terms were favorable. Moreover, transport costs were low because of the development of large tankers and carriers and the concentration of Japanese industries on coastal waters. With government support, Japan built up domestic processing industries to minimize the cost of foreign-supplied materials. The picture has drastically changed with the recent oil crisis, however. The growing assertiveness of raw-material-producing countries, rising prices, and increasing environmental hazards arising from the concentration of industries along the southern coast are all exacerbating the Japanese resource problem.

THE OIL CRISIS

Actions taken in the past several months by the oil-producing countries have produced a serious energy crisis in Japan. Although initial disruptions touched off by the oil embargo and supply cutbacks have been eased somewhat, the dramatic increases in oil prices have greatly aggravated Japan's problems.

Japan imports almost all its oil, with current annual requirements estimated at 1.8 billion barrels. The Arab countries supply 43 percent of Japan's total oil imports, Iran another 40 percent, and Indonesia 12 percent. Japan's oil import bill is expected to rise to about $15 billion in 1974 from $5.7 billion in 1973. At the present level of oil prices, Japan faces in acute form the problem of how to finance the greatly increased foreign exchange costs of its oil imports.

Despite the fact that oil may no longer be a cheap and abundant source of energy, it will continue to be the most important energy source for many years to come. Japan has only minimal fossil fuel resources, and the development of alternative energy sources, such as nuclear power, is at least a decade away. Over the short run, therefore, Japan can do little to reduce its dependence on imported oil except by cutting down on consumption.

Japan's past energy policy was primarily concerned with ensuring the supply of imported energy resources. Now, however, supply stringencies as well as balance-of-payments considerations are causing the conservation of energy to become an essential element of economic policy. This will limit the economy's growth rate and accelerate the structural change that has been under way for some time toward a less energy-intensive economy.

The sobering experience of the current oil crisis is also likely to prompt Japan to undertake a serious reappraisal of its energy supply policy. Although the task of financing its import bill at a much higher price is an immediate problem, the realization that a supply cutoff can be imposed by a small number of oil-producing countries may have much deeper repercussions on the country's energy policy over the longer run. Recent efforts to achieve a degree of national control over the supply of foreign resources are bound to intensify, and increased effort will also be exerted to develop new and substitute sources of energy at home.

OVERSEAS RESOURCE INVESTMENTS

Japan has taken several steps aimed at ensuring access to foreign resources on a stable basis. One method was to extend long-term development loans to foreign mineral producers in return for a commitment to supply materials on a predetermined schedule as repayment of the loans. This practice has been used in copper, iron ore, and coking coal. Although it has brought some degree of stability and afforded protection against price increases, control has been far from complete. Moreover, this method has not afforded Japanese processing firms the opportunity they have sought to participate in the profit associated with upstream (extractive) operations.

Long before their balance-of-payments position strengthened, the Japanese began to expand their direct foreign investments in resource development, including petroleum, copper, iron ore, bauxite, coking coal, and a few other materials. In the case of petroleum, Japan's Arabian Oil Company negotiated for concessions in Kuwait and began producing in 1961. It now supplies about 120 million barrels of crude oil annually. With the success achieved by Arabian Oil, interest in overseas development grew, and oil supplied through Japanese-owned enterprises now accounts for about 10 percent of total crude imports.

The Japanese government has played an important role in encouraging the development of overseas resources. Both Japan's Export-Import Bank and Overseas Economic Cooperation Fund helped to finance overseas investment projects and to provide long-term development loans to foreign mineral producers. Likewise, the government established special financial agencies to provide risk capital to firms engaged in developing foreign resources.

In order to promote resource operations abroad, the Japanese government established the Petroleum Development Corporation and the Metallic Minerals Exploration Agency in 1967. The terms of loans provided by these agencies are highly favorable, with no obligation to repay in the event of failure. Since that time, the number of development projects undertaken by Japanese enterprises has increased to the point where some 150 projects are under way in various parts of the world, including the United States. This trend is likely to accelerate in the light of the stringency in oil supplies experienced in 1973–1974.

To cover one of the major risks of private corporations engaged in foreign resource development, the government also established an investment insurance system that guarantees compensation for losses caused by political upheavals abroad. In addition, resource development projects were given favorable tax treatment in the form of write-offs against losses for special reserves.

The cumulative value of Japanese overseas investment in extractive industries reached about $2.7 billion in 1972, accounting for nearly one-third of the stock of total investment abroad. In recent years, the annual flow has accelerated, reaching $1 billion in 1972, or nearly one-half of Japan's direct overseas investment that year. This pattern is expected to continue for the coming decade, with a concentration in oil, natural gas, coal, iron ore, copper, aluminum, and timber. Geographical distribution is obviously determined by the location of natural resources, but the investments are carefully dispersed into various regions of the world to reduce the potential risk of depending on narrow bases of supply. Japan's investments in the Middle East, Latin America, Oceania, and Southeast Asia consist largely of resource development activities.

THE RESOURCE OUTLOOK

Although Japanese consumption of materials is expected to continue to account for a large proportion of total world requirements, the rate of increase in consumption is likely to diminish in the coming decade. With some slowdown in the growth rate and less emphasis on heavy industries, the Japanese economy will require a smaller volume of materials per unit of tangible output. Also services will bulk larger in total output than during the era of heavy-industry, export-oriented growth.

But even with a moderation in the rate of increase, Japanese consumption will reach a level that may impose a heavy drain on the world's supply of natural resources. According to a pre-crisis forecast, Japan's imports of petroleum and raw materials were expected to account for 25 percent of the world's total trade by 1980.

Japan will confront a number of problems in securing steady supplies of this magnitude. The supply of raw materials does not respond readily to rapid increases in demand. Moreover, supplying countries are increasingly dissatisfied with the terms on which their resources have been developed and exported, and they want a larger voice and a greater return on their development and production. For a number of key minerals, control is exercised by a small number of major international firms, a fact that in the Japanese view intensifies the danger of relying on foreign-controlled sources. In addition, the costs of exploration and development are rising rapidly.

Many informed observers believe that the compelling question in the coming decade is not whether the resources exist but whether the international community will be able to make arrangements to ensure steady flows of resources on a basis that is equitable to both producers and consumers. Despite a rapid increase in consumption, the world's known reserves of most minerals rose during the past decade. There are large areas on earth whose resources are yet to be explored and developed; these include the seabeds, the outer continental shelves, the less accessible regions of the world, as well as some major inland seas. Future uncertainties therefore relate to the adequacy of existing incentives and institutional structures for applying capital, technology, and skilled manpower to the discovery, production, and marketing of materials and to the costs involved in conducting these operations.

INTERNATIONAL COOPERATION IN MATERIALS POLICY

Because of its concern with the growing uncertainties in the world supply of resources, the Japanese government issued its first *White Paper on Natural Resources* in 1971, in which it recommended the development of a comprehensive materials policy. The paper stresses an expansion of overseas investment in resource development to achieve an optimum mix of procurement methods among three alternatives: ordinary imports, long-term purchase contracts, and direct overseas investment. The goal is to step up overseas investment to a level that would supply about one-third of total requirements of petroleum and other key minerals by 1980. Required capital, estimated at $15 billion for the next ten years, will be financed from Japan's huge international monetary reserves.

Development of domestic resources is another important element of the recommended materials policy. Although this is considered un-economic in the short run, it is recognized as in the long-run national interest. Much attention has recently been aroused by new domestic discoveries of graphite and coking coal and by the discovery of natural gas and oil reserves in the vicinity of the home islands.

Because of Japan's growing dependence on overseas resources and its rising share in world trade, Japanese policy on raw materials is certain to have a significant impact on the world materials situation. As other major consumer countries, including the United States, are also becoming increasingly dependent on scarce foreign resources, international competition for supplies may intensify in the future to the detriment of all importing countries. Although the need for cooperation among consuming countries is obvious, Japan has been slow to agree to a joint approach and has expressed a preference for bilateral negotiations in energy matters. As a leading importer, Japan can play a constructive role in promoting various forms of international cooperation, especially with respect to petroleum, where the problems are most critical.

Policy coordination among consumers could be carried out within the OECD, where the Oil Committee has already made a good start. Among the main elements of collaboration would be: forecasting of demand and supply for key raw materials, including energy resources; arrangements for the pooling of supplies in case of emergency; cooperation in research and technology relating to the exploration, development, production, and use of scarce materials; cooperation in financing new undertakings; and a joint effort to work out harmonious relations with producing countries designed to support their development objectives while ensuring steady supplies of materials at reasonable prices.

6. Assistance to Developing Countries

●●●●●●●●●●●●●●●●●●●●●●●●●●●●●●●●●●●

JAPAN'S DEEP INVOLVEMENT with the developing countries is reflected in the huge flow of financial resources to them ($2.7 billion in 1972) as well as in the high proportion of Japan's total trade (more than 40 percent) that takes place with them. The largest deficiency in Japan's relationship with the developing world, however, is the continuing lag in that portion of total financial flows that reflects the true burden of aid, namely, "official development assistance" as defined by OECD's Development Assistance Committee (DAC). In this respect, Japan's contribution as a proportion of GNP falls far behind that of the United States and of the average for DAC countries as a whole. Total financial flows from Japan are high only because of the large proportion of commercial transactions in the form of private investment and export credits.

Japan's official development assistance as a percentage of GNP actually declined in 1972 to 0.21 percent from the 1966–1967 level of about 0.30 percent. The 1972 ratio of 0.21 percent compares with the DAC average of 0.34 percent and 0.29 percent for the United States (see Table 9). Japan is thus even further than other countries from realizing the target of 0.7 percent of GNP in the form of official development assistance, although it stated at UNCTAD that it would make its "utmost efforts" to achieve that target by 1975.

In addition to the low volume of Japan's official development assistance, its terms are harder than the DAC average. Japanese loans bore an average interest rate of 3.5 percent in 1971, as compared with 2.8 percent for the DAC countries as a whole and 2.9 percent for the United States. Japan's loans also carried an average maturity of 22.1 years with a grace period of 6.7 years, as compared with the DAC average maturity of 28.9 years and average grace period of 6.6 years.

A composite measure that comes closest to reflecting the volume of pure assistance to developing countries is the grant equivalent of official development assistance. This measure takes account of differences among donors not only in the volume of this category of aid but in its terms as well. As a percentage of GNP, the grant equivalent of Japan's official development assistance in 1972 was 0.17 percent, as compared with 0.26 percent for the United States and 0.32 percent for DAC countries as a whole.

A charge frequently levied against the Japanese aid program is that commercial considerations take precedence over developmental considerations, as shown by the fact that as recently as 1972, official development assistance amounted to only $611 million out of total flows of $2.7 billion. The bulk of the remainder consisted of export credits and private investment.

A particular problem is caused by export credits, which, because of their short maturities and high interest rates, often seriously aggravate the debt-service problems of those countries where the burden of debt is already heavy. Where debt service cannot be financed out of current export earnings, it is sometimes financed by other loans or grants so that some donor countries find themselves in effect paying, through their official development assistance, to finance other countries' exports.

The problem of debt servicing and its relation to the excessive extension of short-term export credits are matters that require multinational attention and solutions. Japan could make an important contribution to solving the problem by concentrating a much larger proportion of its total financial flows to developing countries in the form of grants and long-term concessionary loans.

One of the characteristics of Japanese economic cooperation has been its heavy concentration in the Asian region. This region accounts for 60 percent of Japan's total flow and almost 80 percent of its official development assistance. Bilateral development assistance has been almost exclusively directed to Asia, with Korea and Indonesia receiving more than half the total. It is understandable that geography as well as economic and

Table 9. ECONOMIC ASSISTANCE BY DAC COUNTRIES TO DEVELOPING COUNTRIES, 1960–1972

	TOTAL OFFICIAL AND PRIVATE FLOWS					OFFICIAL DEVELOPMENT ASSISTANCE				
	1960	1965	1970	1971	1972	1960	1965	1970	1971	1972
MILLIONS OF U.S. DOLLARS										
Total DAC countries	8,115	10,320	15,858	18,285	19,258	4,665	5,916	6,840	7,718	8,613
Japan	246	486	1,824	2,141	2,725	105	244	458	511	611
United States	3,818	5,333	6,254	7,045	7,082	2,707	3,418	3,050	3,324	3,396
France	1,325	1,299	1,835	1,636	2,068	823	752	971	1,088	1,316
West Germany	628	735	1,487	1,915	1,714	223	456	599	734	808
Italy	298	266	682	871	539	77	60	147	183	104
United Kingdom	881	1,032	1,279	1,587	1,696	407	472	447	561	609
PERCENT OF GNP										
Total DAC countries	0.89	0.77	0.80	0.83	0.76	0.52	0.44	0.34	0.35	0.34
Japan	0.57	0.55	0.93	0.95	0.93	0.24	0.28	0.23	0.22	0.21
United States	0.75	0.77	0.64	0.67	0.61	0.53	0.49	0.31	0.32	0.29
France	2.15	1.30	1.24	1.00	1.06	1.38	0.75	0.66	0.67	0.67
West Germany	0.87	0.64	0.80	0.88	0.67	0.31	0.40	0.32	0.34	0.31
Italy	0.85	0.45	0.73	0.86	0.46	0.22	0.10	0.16	0.18	0.09
United Kingdom	1.22	1.03	1.06	1.15	1.11	0.56	0.47	0.37	0.41	0.40

Source: OECD, *Development Cooperation, 1972 Review;* and preliminary data for 1972.

political interests should determine that Japan's largest aid component should go to Asia. In view of Japan's growing world role and broadened economic horizons, however, it would be desirable for Japan to broaden the geographical base of its aid policy.

A strong nationalistic reaction has developed to the high visibility of Japan in the economic life of Southeast Asia. To counter this development, the Japanese government has proposed a new type of program in which its financial assistance would be used to establish local joint ventures with private Japanese companies on a fifty-fifty basis. The program has not yet been favorably received by the governments of Southeast Asia.

The current oil crisis has brought a new dimension to Japan's economic assistance policy. Under pressure of an embargo by Arab oil producers in late 1973, the Japanese government sent out a group of high-level emissaries to persuade the Arab countries to resume shipments. The result has been a promise of loans and grants to these countries exceeding $3 billion in exchange for a stable supply of petroleum. Although not all these commitments would involve official financing, the government portion is likely to be substantial. The funds would be used for the construction of refineries, petrochemical complexes, steel and automobile assembly plants, and giant oil tankers. Japanese government leaders evidently hope that the Middle East will become an important market for Japanese industry. In view of Japan's present deficit in its current account, however, it remains to be seen whether Japan will be able to finance such a large-scale assistance program.

Technical assistance has thus far been a very small element in Japan's economic assistance programs. It amounted to only 1.3 percent ($36 million) of total aid funds in 1972 and 5.8 percent of official development assistance. The Japanese face special problems in bringing technical assistance to Asian countries where suspicion and hostility still exist on the part of people whose countries were occupied by Japanese troops during World War II. In some countries, the Japanese still have a long way to go to work their way back into full acceptance and to win the confidence of the local people. Recruitment of qualified personnel in Japan is also difficult. Because of the shortage of skilled labor and the tradition of lifetime employment and the rigidity of the Japanese industrial system, few technicians are willing to take up temporary service overseas at possible sacrifice of long-term careers at home. Language is also often a formidable obstacle to the effectiveness of the Japanese technical expert.

In spite of these problems, Japan recognizes the importance of expanding its technical aid programs, as evidenced by the establishment of the International Development Center of Japan in 1972. Japanese specialists can make major contributions in fields in which they have shown outstanding competence, including agriculture, fisheries, industry, mining, and health.

Promotion of imports from developing countries constitutes an important element of international assistance policy. Japan initiated its preferential tariff system for imports from developing countries in August 1971 following similar action by the European Community. Since then, the list of beneficiary countries has been expanded and the coverage of commodities widened.

At the end of 1972, beneficiaries of Japan's preference scheme included 106 countries and 18 territories, covering almost the entire developing world. The list of commodities included 59 agricultural products (on a Brussels Tariff Nomenclature four-digit basis) and those manufactured goods not subject to Japan's residual import quotas. For manufactured products subject to preferences, ceilings are placed on total imports allowed at the preferential tariff rates, the ceiling on each item being determined by the base year (1968) imports from developing countries plus a certain percentage addition. Imports from any one country may not exceed 50 percent of the total amount of the ceiling on each item. The rates of tariff reductions under the preference system vary, ranging from 20 to 100 percent.

During the brief period that the scheme has been in effect, its benefits have been rather limited. Despite some recent liberalization, the quota ceiling remains low for many products. To accommodate an increasing flow of imports from developing countries, Japan will have to continue to take vigorous action to promote structural adjustments in domestic industries. Severe competition from developing countries is already taking place in a number of labor-intensive industries. Continued high growth rates in Japan and an active industrial policy on the part of the government should go a long way to facilitate those changes within Japan that will accommodate the products of developing countries in a more rational international division of labor.

7. Balance-of-Payments Adjustment Policy

••••••••••••••••••••••••••••

Until 1968, Japan's economic policies had been constrained by the precariousness of its foreign exchange position. Between 1968 and 1972, the position shifted to one of ever-increasing surplus and embarrassingly large foreign exchange reserves. Although this change freed Japan from the balance-of-payments constraints that had long conditioned its domestic and foreign economic policy making, the increasing surpluses brought about a new set of acute problems in its external economic relations. In 1973, however, the situation changed dramatically as the surplus disappeared and a floating rate was adopted for the yen. In this chapter, trends in Japan's balance of payments during the last two decades, policies followed to deal with them, and the outlook for the rest of the decade will be examined.

TREND AND STRUCTURE
OF JAPAN'S BALANCE OF PAYMENTS

Until the mid-1960s, the Japanese economy had experienced repeated balance-of-payments crises. The chronic deficit in the merchandise trade account was a basic factor underlying Japan's payments difficulties. Imports of current services also exceeded exports of services (excluding government transactions consisting primarily of receipts from the U.S. military

74

establishment in Japan), making the total deficit in current private transactions even greater than the trade deficit. The largest deficit item in the
service account was payments for shipping and insurance. Interest and
dividends to foreign investors and royalties and fees for technology and
management services were also net payment items.

The tendency toward deficit in private current transactions did not,
however, always mean a loss of foreign exchange reserves. American military expenditures provided a substantial supplement to foreign exchange
earnings, particularly during the Korean and Vietnam wars. In addition,
Japan received a large flow of loans and investments, mostly from the
United States. But Japan's foreign exchange reserves were subject to
fluctuations that at times brought the country close to international
insolvency.

The basic factor underlying the turnaround in 1968 was, of course,
the improvement in Japan's trade balance. For years, exports had been
growing faster than imports. From 1953 to the mid-1960s, Japanese exports increased at the rate of over 16 percent per year while imports grew
at about 13 percent. As explained earlier, this disparity was fundamentally
an outcome of Japan's growth strategy, which included improvement of
the competitiveness of the country's exports while at the same time reducing its dependence on imports.

In addition to these developments in merchandise trade, changes
have occurred in the service accounts that have contributed to the overall
improvement. Aided by government subsidies, the domestic shipping industry assumed an increasing share of the transportation of Japan's foreign
trade. Japanese investment income also grew faster than payments on
foreign borrowing as Japan's overseas investments expanded rapidly. As
progress was made in the development of an indigenous technological
capability, external payments for technology and management services
decelerated.

Parallel to the development of a current account surplus, Japan's
long-term capital account has also changed from a position of net importer
to that of net exporter. Between 1965 and 1971, net long-term capital
outflow was about $5 billion, and another $5 billion was invested abroad
in 1972 alone. This flow reflects Japan's growing interest in direct investment abroad, particularly in overseas resource development. A large part
of the outflow was also in the form of export credits and an increasing flow
of long-term loans to developing countries.

By 1971, it became clear that Japan's balance-of-payments surplus
was not merely a brief respite from its old deficit position (see Table 10).

It was fundamentally a new problem that required urgent corrective action from both the domestic and international points of view. For the Japanese, the growing surpluses meant a waste of precious resources in the piling up of idle foreign exchange reserves, resources that could be used for improving domestic welfare, social overhead capital, and other long-neglected needs. For the world as a whole, the continued large imbalances signified a failure of the international adjustment mechanism and contributed to doubts about the viability of an international monetary system based on the dollar as a reserve currency.

In a multilateral world, no particular significance should attach to purely bilateral payments relationships. As a practical matter, however, the balance of payments between the United States and Japan was a focus of acute tension. More than one-half of Japan's $6 billion current account surplus in 1971 was accounted for by its surplus with the United States, and in 1972 the proportion became even larger. The deficit of the United States in its merchandise trade with Japan alone amounted to $3.2 billion in 1971, more than the overall U.S. trade deficit of about $2.7 billion for that year. In viewing similar figures, the United States tended to see much of its own balance-of-payments difficulty in terms of its deficit with Japan. In the end, it was America's initiative with respect to its own payments crises in 1971 and 1973 that dictated the timing of both instances of Japan's revaluation of the yen.

In 1973, Japan's basic payments position swung into a deficit of $10 billion, a deterioration of $12 billion from the previous year. Export growth slowed substantially while imports expanded at an unusually high rate. Several factors were responsible for this dramatic turnaround on the trade side: the cumulative upward revaluation of the yen since 1971, strong domestic growth during 1973, the government's export-restraint and import-stimulation policy, and rapid increases in the prices of oil and other basic imported commodities. As a result, Japan's trade surplus (on an f.o.b. basis) declined from $9 billion in the previous year to $3.8 billion in 1973.

Another important factor in the turnaround was the rapidly expanding net outflow of Japanese long-term capital. In fact, the deficit on the long-term capital account was equal to the overall deficit of about $10 billion. Japan's capital outflow was a response to the government's stimulus to overseas investment as well as to the cumulative appreciation of the yen that made foreign assets cheap.

A major question is the impact of the steep increase in crude oil prices, the full impact of which will show up in Japan's 1974 import

Table 10. JAPAN'S BALANCE OF PAYMENTS, 1962–1973   (*billions of dollars*)

	Total					With United States			
	1962	1970	1971	1972	1973[a]	1970	1971	1972	1973[a]
Trade balance	0.4	4.0	7.8	9.0	3.8	1.2	3.2	4.1	1.3
Exports (f.o.b.)	4.9	19.0	23.6	28.1	36.2	5.9	7.3	9.1	9.6
Imports (f.o.b.)	4.5	15.0	15.8	19.1	32.4	4.6	4.1	5.0	8.3
Invisible trade balance	-0.4	-1.8	-1.7	-1.9	-3.5	0.3	0.2	0.6	0.4
Receipts	1.1	4.0	4.8	6.2	8.4	1.5	1.7	2.4	2.1
Payments	1.5	5.8	6.6	8.1	11.9	1.3	1.5	1.7	1.7
Transfers, net	(X)	-0.2	-0.3	-0.5	-0.3	(X)	(X)	(X)	(X)
Current account balance	-0.2	2.0	5.8	6.7	-0.1	1.5	3.4	4.8	1.7
Long-term capital, net	0.1	-1.6	-1.1	-4.5	-9.7	(X)	0.9	-0.3	-1.1
Basic balance	-0.1	0.4	4.7	2.3	-9.8	1.6	4.3	4.5	0.6

Sources: Bank of Japan, for total balance of payments; and U.S. Department of Commerce, for balance of payments with the United States.

[a] Preliminary data.

(X) Indicates less than $50 million.

figures. The government estimates that the value of imports of crude and refined petroleum products will just about double in fiscal 1974 from the $8.5 billion in 1973 on the assumption of no change in the volume of imports. To counter the increase of almost $9 billion in petroleum imports, the Japanese government hopes to achieve a rapid rise in exports while containing the increase in imports other than petroleum to perhaps 5 percent (in part because of the expected slowdown in the economy). In addition, the net outflow of long-term capital is expected to be substantially reduced because of a switch from policies designed to contract Japan's foreign currency holdings. Despite the increase in oil prices, therefore, the government expects Japan's basic balance to improve in 1974 over what it was in 1973.

Japan's efforts to reduce its nonessential imports and to expand its exports could lead to new strains in its relations with other countries, which also must cope with higher oil-import prices. This is particularly true of Japan's relationship with the United States, which constitutes Japan's principal export market as well as its major source of nonoil imports.

MECHANISMS OF BALANCE-OF-PAYMENTS ADJUSTMENT

Under a par value system, policy instruments available for dealing with a balance-of-payments deficit may take several forms: internal measures (monetary and fiscal policies) to control aggregate demand; external measures to shift demand by controlling foreign trade and capital movements; financing the deficit by foreign credit; and a change in the exchange rate. The Japanese have traditionally relied primarily on monetary policy to deal with balance-of-payments crises, although they have also made extensive use of trade and capital controls. Historically, they have been reluctant to depend on capital flows from abroad to finance current deficits, nor until recently have they regarded exchange rate changes as an appropriate means of adjustment as long as other choices existed.

Internal Measures for Adjustment. In the 1952-to-1972 period, Japan experienced four balance-of-payments crises: 1953, 1957, 1961, and 1965. Each time, an overexpansion in the domestic economy produced strains on international reserves to which the monetary authority responded with a restrictive monetary policy. The modus operandi of the process of balance-of-payments adjustment during this period may be summed up as follows: when a business boom led to excessive private investment, imports would increase much faster than exports, and the balance of payments would start to deteriorate. When foreign exchange reserves fell to a critical point, the central bank would apply the monetary brakes. High rates of interest and tight credit rationing discouraged business investment, and economic growth slowed down. With the slower pace of growth, the volume of imports would moderate, and the external balance would improve. As the central bank relaxed its restrictive policy, the level of investment would begin to rise again.

In Chapter 2, two important features of the Japanese financial structure were described that contributed to the success of monetary policy: a heavy dependence on commercial banks by business firms for their investment funds and a continuous debt of the banking system to the central bank. Although monetary policy has been the primary means of adjustment, restrictive fiscal policy has rarely been used for the purpose of correcting balance-of-payments disequilibriums. Insofar as fiscal policy was used as a tool for managing aggregate demand, it was applied primarily to the long-term objective of maintaining a high rate of economic growth.

The changed situation in the balance of payments in recent years has presented a new challenge for Japan's fiscal and monetary policy making. In 1969, when booming demand and price conditions at home called for a restrictive monetary policy, the existence of a large balance-of-payments surplus led, for the first time, to a conflict between domestic and external objectives. It was feared that tight money would accelerate an inflow of foreign short-term capital and hence further enlarge the payments surplus. Furthermore, there have been signs that the response of business investment to changes in monetary policy has become slower, pointing to the desirability of supplementing monetary with fiscal measures for adjustment purposes. Progressive liberalization of government policy on foreign capital has also made the task of monetary policy more difficult. Under these circumstances, more active use of fiscal policy has become more desirable. Indeed, such a trend should be facilitated by the government's recent heavy resort to the private bond market to finance its stepped-up budgetary expenditures for social infrastructure.

Measures to Control Trade and Capital Flows. Until the early 1960s, direct measures to control trade and capital movements had been rather extensively used by Japan to affect the balance of payments and to safeguard the country's meager reserves. After Japan joined IMF and GATT in the mid-1960s, it came under much more severe constraints with respect to the imposition or retention of restrictions on trade or capital flows for balance-of-payments reasons. As Japan began to dismantle import quotas and exchange controls, the direct measures taken explicitly to deal with short-run balance-of-payments deficits took the form of suspension or slowdown in the ongoing schedule of liberalization. As a result, the link between restrictions and balance-of-payments policy became less clear. Nevertheless, the scope and rapidity of the liberalization had a significant impact on the evolving structure of Japan's balance of payments. The delay in liberalization undoubtedly contributed to the emergence of long-term structural imbalances between Japan and its major trading partners.

Exchange Rate Policy and the Yen Revaluations. Before the Nixon administration acted in August 1971, Japan attempted to meet its new situation of mounting balance-of-payments surpluses with a variety of measures short of revaluation of the yen. Liberalization of imports and outward capital movements was speeded up, and special incentives for exports were reduced or eliminated. When Japan was pressed to revalue, its leaders responded that their complicated system of controls (erected to handle the old balance-of-payments deficit problem) must be dismantled first. They also argued that internal measures aimed at increasing aggregate demand and improving domestic resource allocation would increase imports and help to bring about a large part of the needed adjustment. These various measures were brought together in June 1971 in an Eight Point Program for Avoiding Yen Revaluation.

By that time, however, it was becoming clear that this type of program could not cope with the mounting surplus on the scale or with the rapidity that was required. Revaluation of the yen appeared inevitable. In August 1971, the United States suspended the convertibility of the dollar and temporarily imposed a 10 percent surcharge on all dutiable imports in an attempt to force its trading partners to undertake sizable revaluations immediately. After months of negotiation and as part of a multilateral agreement reached in December 1971, a new official rate of 308 yen per U.S. dollar became effective, representing a 16.88 percent upward revaluation of the yen.

The currency realignment achieved in December 1971 prevented a general breakdown of the international payments system. But it was intended only as a holding operation that would provide time for a more fundamental reform of the international monetary system to be worked out. So long as large surpluses and deficits could cumulate in the balance of payments of major countries, an atmosphere of instability remained in international trade and payments relations. Persistent differences in growth rates and wage increases among major industrial countries and the attendant rapid structural changes among them clearly required a high degree of flexibility in the mechanism of exchange rate adjustment.

Despite the 17 percent revaluation of the yen late in 1971, Japan's trade surplus widened in 1972 to about $9 billion. A combination of factors contributed to dampening the response to the revaluation. In the first place, a large proportion of exports shipped after the revaluation had already been arranged before December 1971 in anticipation of a revaluation. Japan was also able to increase its exports to countries where the revaluation did not change local currency prices significantly because of upward revaluations in those countries as well.

The most important factor, however, in frustrating the effects of the yen revaluation was the Japanese distribution system. A trading company often served as the sole distributor of an imported product. Instead of reducing the yen price of the imported product by an amount proportional to the exchange rate change, the trading company simply increased its profit margin. At the same time, the company used the high profits on imports to subsidize Japanese exports, thereby offsetting the effects of the revaluation on the export side.

The Japanese trading companies were able to operate in this way because of their monopolistic position as sole distributors for many American products. Although the sole-importer system is breaking down, the process of dismantling it should be accelerated. American exporters should be free to sell to any distributor or even directly to major Japanese retail outlets. As mentioned earlier, U.S. firms should be free to establish their own retail outlets in Japan without restriction.

Because of the sluggishness of the impact of exchange rate changes on trade flows, the government adopted a new program late in 1972 for reducing Japan's surpluses despite the failure of earlier measures to produce satisfactory results. The program included: measures to expand imports, including a uniform 20 percent cut in tariffs on imports of finished goods and an expansion of the current quota limitations on restricted items; measures to restrain exports, including export restrictions under the Export Trade Control Ordinance and the termination of remaining tax incentives for exports such as overseas market development reserves; further relaxation of foreign exchange controls on the outflow of capital; untying of major elements of Japan's foreign aid program and a liberalization of quota limitations on preferential tariffs on imports from developing countries.

Adoption of the 1972 program was designed to stop the burgeoning surplus and thus to avert a second revaluation of the yen. But few realists believed it would have a significant effect. The prevailing feeling was that it was again a matter of too little and too late. Given Japan's trade surplus of $9 billion, imports would have to rise one-and-a-half times as fast as exports simply to prevent the absolute size of the surplus from increasing. Anything short of a second revaluation appeared to most observers as another case of temporizing that could lead to further protectionist moves on the part of Japan's trading partners as well as other adverse consequences for the international economic system generally.

Revaluation not only failed to result in a rapid adjustment of the trade balance but also failed to induce an outflow of the foreign capital that had entered Japan, despite the country's exchange controls, in anticipation of a revaluation. Evidently, speculators were convinced that the 1971 revaluation was insufficient, and their expectations were fulfilled in the further currency realignments and floating that followed the massive flight from the dollar in early February 1973.

The general move by major industrial countries to floating rates was followed by some wide fluctuations and divergent movements among the major currencies. Nevertheless, the yen remained relatively stable until the current world oil crisis began to disrupt the international payments mechanism. The weakening of the yen as well as other major currencies against the dollar was influenced by the prevailing view of the international exchange markets that Japan and Europe would suffer far more than the United States as a result of the increase in oil prices and the supply disruptions. The gradual improvement in the U.S. balance of payments during 1973 also contributed to strengthening the dollar. Current exchange rates cannot be regarded as stable, however, until the uncertainties surrounding the world oil situation subside. Nevertheless, the move to generalized floating was fortunate in that the disruptions caused by the abrupt and drastic changes in oil prices would undoubtedly have been much more severe under a fixed rate system.

OUTLOOK FOR JAPAN'S BALANCE OF PAYMENTS

As noted earlier, after five years of increasing surpluses, Japan's balance of payments shifted into deficit in 1973. The most serious immediate problem is, of course, to find ways to deal with the dramatic increase in oil prices. The sudden appearance of this new factor, with the uncertainty it entails, necessarily limits the validity and utility of any discussion about the longer-term payments outlook. It may be useful, however, to see how the prospects appeared before the present oil crisis occurred. This at least provides a view of how the underlying forces would have affected the trend, as well as a starting point for drawing new conclusions once the effects of the oil price increases on the international payments system become clearer.

Few exercises in economic forecasting are as fraught with uncertainty as projections of a country's payments position. The United States has rarely been able to predict its own balance of payments with any degree of accuracy even one year ahead. To venture beyond a year or two is entering the realm of the unknown. One reason is that a country's payments position, however defined, is a residual: small percentage movements in the major underlying variables can and do yield greatly magnified changes in the residual. Moreover, changes in the major components themselves depend on developments and policy changes not only in the country concerned but in its principal trading and investing partners as well. The normal uncertainty is now compounded by the major changes pending in the international trade and monetary systems.

On the assumption that a high degree of exchange rate flexibility will be an essential feature of whatever system emerges from the current international monetary negotiations, the outlook for Japan's balance of payments reduces itself to the question of the prospects for the exchange value of the yen. Can it be assumed that at the current rate a stable equilibrium has been reached in the sense that no further significant reserve accumulation by Japan (and possibly some drawdown) will take place over the period to 1980? Or are there forces at work propelling Japan toward a resumption of either the deficit position faced until the middle 1960s or the persistent surplus position that prevailed from 1968 to 1972? Either situation would be resolvable only through further changes in the exchange value of the yen.

There is no crystal ball that would provide a definitive answer to this question. On the one hand, a strong case can be made for the view that after a brief period Japan will again exert the balance-of-payments pressures of a country in a structural surplus position. The upward revaluation of the yen has changed the static cost and price relationships between Japan and the rest of the world, but the underlying trends that brought about the disequilibrium in the first place may well persist.

According to this view, Japan's productivity gains will continue to outpace those of its trading partners. Despite some slowdown, the rate of investment embodying technological innovation will continue at high levels by Western standards. Nor are the habits of hard work of Japan's labor force and the skill and imagination of its entrepreneurs likely to erode significantly over the remaining years of the decade. At the same time, cost and price pressures in export industries are likely to remain less intense than in other countries because of the discipline of Japan's labor force and the possibility of satisfying its desire for economic improvement through large real-wage increases that do not exceed the gains in productivity. In short, as long as Japan's productivity grows faster than that of its trading partners while the pressures of rising costs remain more moderate, the United States and others are bound to experience a resumption of strong pressures from Japan stemming from large trade and current account surpluses. Although long-term capital outflows associated with the multinationalization of Japanese firms will continue at high levels, they are unlikely to offset fully the surpluses on current account.

The contrary view lays prime stress on forces tending to arrest Japan's rapid economic growth rate and to intensify pressures on prices. Among the former are the narrowing technological gap between Japan and the West and the reordering of national priorities in favor of larger allocations of capital to housing and social overhead projects as contrasted with directly productive investment in tradable goods. On the side of costs, emphasis is placed on the recent acceleration of wage increases in Japan and the steeply rising cost of imported fuel and raw materials on which Japan is almost totally dependent. These factors may be expected to bring the long-term trend in Japan's wholesale prices more in line with that of other countries. Additional considerations arguing against the re-emergence of a large Japanese trade surplus in the remaining years of the decade are the import liberalization measures of the early seventies and the likelihood that foreign producers will exert much greater efforts in the future to penetrate the vast Japanese market for manufactured goods. Finally, to the extent that some Japanese surplus on trade account persists, it is likely to be offset by a stepped-up level of long-term foreign investments.

8. Conclusions

● ●

In this concluding chapter, two subjects will be addressed briefly: lessons for the United States in Japan's growth experience and the changing thrust of Japan's foreign economic policy.

LESSONS FOR THE UNITED STATES

Any assessment of Japan's economic performance must be tempered by the now widely acknowledged social costs, economic distortions, and environmental desecration that have accompanied that country's unparalleled growth. However, one cannot but be struck by the magnitude of Japan's achievement reflected in a sustained increase in real per capita GNP of 8.7 percent per annum over the period from 1955 to 1972. In the light of the gulf between this growth rate and the comparable figure of 2.2 percent for the United States, it is natural to ask what lessons can be learned from the Japanese experience.

The first observation is that this whole subject is fraught with pitfalls. It is all too easy to fall into the trap of ascribing rapid growth to whatever is different in the Japanese experience and to propose that the United States should go ahead and do likewise. It has been suggested, for example, that the lifetime employment system has contributed in various ways to increasing productivity by engendering a sense of loyalty to the firm and by generating greater personal satisfaction on the job. On the other hand, the system may also have had opposite effects, such as reducing labor mobility and engendering a sense of complacency in the work force. It would be difficult to strike a balance between those opposing tendencies, but it is at least possible that the growth of output in Japan would have been even more rapid if the employment system had conformed more closely to the pattern prevailing in the West. Even if it could be established that such special features of the Japanese economy had a great deal to do with the country's growth performance, it would still not follow that they could be transplanted in whole or in part to a country whose history, traditions, and culture are so different from those of Japan.

Another point to bear in mind is that some of the basic factors underlying Japan's spectacular economic performance were dependent upon opportunities associated with that country's position as a latecomer to the modernization process. The vast shifts of labor supply from low-productivity agriculture to the industrial sectors that characterized Japan's growth in the period from 1950 to 1970 obviously cannot serve as a pattern for a mature economy such as the United States, where the agricultural labor force has already declined to about 4 percent. Nor can the United States, as a country in the forefront of research and development, expect to follow on anything like a comparable scale the Japanese pattern of acquiring existing foreign technology cheaply, taking advantage of the fact that the main costs were borne by others.

In addition to the role of technology and sector shifts in explaining Japan's growth, a major factor has been the high rate of investment. Gross domestic capital formation averaged over 30 percent in Japan as compared with about 18 percent for the United States over the period from 1950 to 1971. Here, too, however, the possible lesson for the United States cannot be taken at face value. The comparison does not connote, quite to the extent that some have suggested, that Americans have lived excessively well while the Japanese have sacrificed and saved to devote a larger proportion of their output to productive investment. In the period from 1950 to 1970, 9 percent of U.S. GNP was allocated to defense expenditures as compared with about 1 percent for Japan. The difference of 8 percent, when added to U.S. investment, substantially reduces the gap between nonconsumption expenditures in the United States and Japan. The lesson remains, however, that a higher growth rate calls for a higher rate of investment.

Nothing that has been said above is meant to detract from the tremendous achievement of the Japanese in mobilizing and utilizing effectively the productive resources available to them and in adopting policies at the governmental level favorable to the realization of the outstanding entrepreneurial qualities of Japan's business leaders and the capacity of the Japanese people in general for hard and sustained work. What is difficult and frankly frustrating, however, is the effort to draw from the Japanese experience implications for U.S. policy. Therefore, only a few tentative observations are offered.

The first is that serious thought ought to be given to whether Japan's pragmatic policy toward industrial concentration may be more appropriate to modern conditions than the American approach, which takes its shape essentially from legislation and policies reflecting conditions around the turn of the twentieth century. Here the reference is not to cartels and other restrictive business practices among business firms but only to the question of industrial concentration. Has American policy on concentration been directed to preserving competition or to protecting particular competitors? If a case can be made for mergers or joint ventures on the basis of greater technological efficiency, more rational operations, and improved international competitiveness, should present constraints based on market shares be relaxed? In a day of multinational corporations and increasing ratios of trade to GNP, how relevant is it to look at size in terms of shares of the domestic market alone? In short, it would seem that the time has come for a careful study of the social and economic costs and benefits of a less rigid policy toward industrial mergers and concentration.

The second point relates to the way in which the Japanese government has stimulated growth by encouraging high rates of investment and technological innovation. Actually, the two are closely related since business expenditures for plant and equipment contribute to enhanced productivity not only directly but also as the vehicle through which much of the new technology is introduced.

One way in which the Japanese government has stimulated private investment is by keeping its own claim on the national output at a low level, largely because of its minimal expenditures on defense and social security. In these respects, it is, of course, neither desirable nor feasible for the United States to attempt to emulate the Japanese experience. In addition, however, the government has pursued a conscious policy of promoting investment by ensuring the availability of funds for this purpose through the banking system on highly favorable terms and by a variety of financial measures, including reductions in the corporate income tax, special reserves for abnormal risks, and rapid depreciation allowances for industries deemed to be strategic for the country's growth objectives.

To the extent that the United States regards as a desirable objective a more rapid growth in output than the 2.2 percent per capita that it has achieved since 1955, it will need to consider seriously ways of according higher priority to investment incentives and their concomitant stimulus to technological innovation. For this purpose, closer study of Japanese experience in monetary and tax policy would appear to be warranted.

The last point relates to the role of government in improving the process of sectoral adjustment in response to today's rapid shifts in conditions of demand and supply, particularly shifts induced by changing patterns of international trade. Looking at the experience of the last decade or so, one is struck by the contrast between the active policy of the Japanese government and what can only be described as the protective but basically passive role of the U.S. government. Not only has the Japanese government been aggressive in targeting and encouraging the establishment and growth of new and dynamic industries of high capital intensity and advanced technology, it has also actively encouraged and assisted the process of phasing out declining industries (e.g., coal after the switch in policy toward the importation of oil in 1949) or upgrading and rationalizing those industries whose international competitiveness had weakened (e.g., textile spinning and weaving in 1966 and 1967 and the knitting, dyeing, and finishing industries in 1969). By contrast, the main elements of U.S. policy have consisted of the protection of import-vulnerable industries through formal or informal import restrictions, as in some textiles, steel, and flatware (adopted originally as temporary measures but in practice highly persistent) and through so-called adjustment assistance to workers, which has rarely consisted of anything beyond supplementary unemployment insurance.

In facilitating adjustment to change, there is also a lesson in Japanese employers' lifetime commitment to employees (noted earlier), in which there is a readier acceptance of change. It is in the interest of U.S. employers to preserve for employees—who are required to change jobs— their seniority and pension, health, and other benefits. Society's interest should be great enough to underwrite the costs of transfer and retraining. There may also be advantages to providing easier and cheaper access to capital for growth industries of high productivity as a means of providing new jobs for those that are lost in less competitive activities.

In short, it would seem essential today for the United States to devise and adopt more comprehensive and effective policies for lubricating the shift in industrial structure in line with a more rational international division of labor. At the same time, it is only fair to recognize that the task of facilitating sectoral shifts in a modern economy is much easier in a setting in which total output has been growing more or less steadily at 10 percent annually than in one in which the growth rate averages less than 4 percent.

CHANGING THRUST OF
JAPAN'S FOREIGN ECONOMIC POLICY

Within the single decade through 1972, Japan not only raised its per capita GNP from one-fifth that of the United States to one-half but also succeeded in converting its international economic position from one of persistent balance-of-payments deficits to one of steadily increasing surplus. But until very recently, economic policies and attitudes in Japan still bore the mark of the early postwar atmosphere of internal privation and external dependence and vulnerability. Many of the problems and tensions in the economic relations between Japan and the United States have been aggravated by this gap between the reality of Japan's economic strength and vitality and a set of inward-looking and defensive policies geared to the circumstances of an earlier period.

A significant shift has been taking place recently, however, in the Japanese approach to international economic policy, Increasingly, Japan has opened its economy to foreign trade and investment and has shown a willingness to take positive steps toward making the international economic system work. Although many of these measures were adopted under strong pressure from the United States and other countries, one senses a growing conviction in Japan that a liberal international economic policy is in its own interest.

Perhaps of greatest significance is Japan's shift in the monetary field from a rigid defense of a highly undervalued yen to a grudging appreciation of its currency and finally to an acceptance today of the need not only for substantial flexibility in the exchange rate mechanism but also for symmetrical adjustment obligations on the part of surplus and deficit countries. Characteristically, however, Japan has put forward no plan of its own for international monetary reform, and its posture has been one of passive cooperation rather than active leadership.

In the field of trade policy, Japan has come a long way toward eliminating the complex of restrictions on imports and special government aids to exports that for many years have insulated its home market while stimulating its producers to penetrate foreign markets. Today Japan's tariffs are comparable in level with those of other industrial countries. The only significant industrial products still under quota are computers, integrated circuits, and leather goods, and a timetable has been established for removing import curbs on integrated circuits and computers. Special tax and other incentives for exports have been all but eliminated; the only ones remaining are for small and financially weak enterprises.

Looking to the future, Japan may well emerge as the world's leading proponent of liberal trade policies. Given the country's almost total dependence on imports for raw materials and its heavy reliance on overseas supplies of basic food and feedstuffs, it is not surprising that Japan perceives its interest in terms of an open world trading system, open not only in terms of unimpeded access to foreign sources of materials but also in terms of access to export markets needed to finance those essential imports and to sustain demand for the country's high-growth industries. Until recently, however, Japan's own protectionist policies placed it in a weak position to press for the elimination of other countries' trade restrictions. Now that Japan has progressed far in liberalizing its own policies, it is in a much stronger position to espouse a new set of trade rules that would put pressure on all countries to reduce barriers and especially to get rid of quantitative restrictions and other nontariff distortions that in many cases have been directed specifically against Japan.

In this context, two sets of trade restrictions have had a special impact on Japan. One consists of discriminatory import quotas still applied against many Japanese goods by individual members of the European Community on the basis of bilateral agreements dating from the early 1960s. Apart from their trade impact, these restrictions are particularly onerous because they reflect the continued unwillingness of a number of countries to accept Japan as a full-fledged member of the world trading community entitled to treatment equal to that of other countries.

The other set of restrictions comprised the U.S. export controls on soybeans and various other agricultural products imposed briefly during 1973. To many in Japan, these restrictions came as a fourth Nixon shock. As a result of vigorous U.S. promotional efforts and the phasing down of Japanese restrictions, Japan had become the American farmer's biggest customer. Japanese self-sufficiency in soybeans had been reduced from 28 percent in 1960 to only 3 percent in 1972, with the United States supplying 90 percent of the soybeans consumed in Japan. As with the other Nixon shocks, what was most disturbing to the Japanese was not so much the idea of allocating supplies to deal with a temporary worldwide shortage but the unilateralism (despite pro forma advance consultation) of an action that affected them so profoundly. At the July 1973 session of the cabinet-level Joint Japan-U.S. Committee on Trade and Economic Affairs, the problems posed by the U.S. export controls tended to overshadow the customary complaints about residual import controls by Japan. It would be surprising, indeed, if Japan did not take the lead in pressing in the forthcoming negotiations for some internationalization of the process of resource allocation in times of scarcity.

Despite Japan's substantial import liberalization, two features of Japanese economic policy remain significant inhibitors of trade, even though they are not included in the conventional listings of import restrictions. One is the practice of administrative guidance by the government (described earlier). Given the close business-government relationship in Japan, this informal practice can be a major distorter of the international market mechanism, yet it is quite unreachable by the usual type of trade rules that focus on formal, official acts of government. An effort will have to be made within the framework of the forthcoming trade negotiations to come to grips with this problem.

The second trade inhibitor is the continued restriction of foreign investment in retail trade operations. Despite the epoch-making fifth round of liberalization of inward foreign investment in May 1973, retail trade continues as one of the handful of nonliberalized categories and one of the exceptions to the newly established principle of allowing 100 percent foreign ownership. Given the archaic and fragmented nature of the Japanese distribution system, direct investment in retailing may be the most effective way or in some cases the only feasible way for American firms to reach the Japanese consumer.

The alleged Japanese justification for nonliberalization of retailing is put in terms of the social consequences of excessively rapid displacement of existing small enterprises in what is generally regarded as the most backward sector of the Japanese economy. It is difficult to understand, however, why this social concern justifies differentiating between Japanese and foreign investors rather than applying nondiscriminatory restrictions, since displacement of small shopkeepers would occur regardless of the nationality of investors in large-scale, modern retail operations. This is an area in which Japanese policy continues to lag behind that of other industrial countries and in which continued discrimination against foreign operations is bound to remain a source of international tension.

Despite the exception of retailing and four other fields, however,

Japan has come a long way in liberalizing foreign investment in the past several years. Among the sweeping changes introduced in the fifth round was the removal of the stringent restrictions on the acquisition of existing enterprises. Given the historical Japanese fear of compromising their national independence and the consequent opposition to foreign ownership and control of Japanese industries dating back to the early Meiji era, the recent moves mark a major break with past policy.

As in the case of trade liberalization, however, the long-overdue steps with respect to foreign investment were partly a response to strong pressures from abroad, particularly from the United States, and partly a result of the redefinition of Japan's own interest as a major power in the world economy. Prominent in the latter regard is Japan's emergence as a major foreign investor itself, with net long-term capital outflows in 1973 amounting to almost $10 billion. Japan realizes that its freedom to maintain and develop that role would be undermined by restrictive policies on foreign investment at home.

Japan's own overseas investment performs a strategic function in its economy. On the macro level, Japan views overseas investment as the principal means of reconciling possible large recurrent future trade surpluses with equilibrium in its balance of payments. On the micro level, foreign investment serves a number of purposes: as a major vehicle for ensuring stable supplies of fuel and raw materials at reasonable cost; as a means of escape from the domestic constraints imposed by environmental pollution, a shortage of land for industrial sites, and a tight and costly supply of labor; and as a means of retaining overseas markets in the face of import substitution policies adopted by the host countries. Because of these interests, Japan may be expected to exert strong efforts to reduce tensions arising in the field of foreign investment. Particularly in developing countries, where nearly half of Japanese overseas direct investment is located, Japanese firms are likely to try to accommodate to a greater extent than in the past to national sensitivities about foreign political and economic domination.

The current worldwide scarcity and escalating prices of petroleum and raw materials have dramatized Japan's vulnerability as a country so heavily dependent on foreign-controlled sources of supply. Under present circumstances, Japan no longer regards as adequate its traditional policy of relying on open-market purchases supplemented occasionally by long-term contracts. Today, Japan has both the capability and the determination to invest directly in the development and exploitation of natural resources abroad as a means of assuring greater security of supplies at reasonable prices. Although these activities are carried out on private initiative, the government plays an important role as a catalyst and as a financial source.

With respect to petroleum in particular, Japan may be expected to seek to maintain harmonious relations with the producing states while at the same time engaging in various forms of cooperation with other major importing countries. In the latter category are arrangements for sharing oil in times of emergency, joint efforts for exploring and exploiting energy sources in the Soviet Union and elsewhere, and cooperation in research and development of new energy sources.

Throughout the postwar period, Japan has concentrated on internal reconstruction and economic growth while maintaining a low profile in the field of international politics. For its own security, it has relied on the U.S. nuclear umbrella and the Seventh Fleet, along with a minimum domestic force based on conventional weapons for the defense of the home islands. Although some upgrading of Japanese military forces is being planned, it is apparent that the Japanese government has rejected the nuclear option and will continue to rely for its ultimate defense on its security relationship with the United States.

The United States understands the complex of internal and international considerations that underlie this policy and believes it will serve the interests of both countries by contributing to stability and avoiding new tensions in Asia and the Far East. At the same time, the policy does imply in economic terms a continuation of the sharp discrepancy between the burden of defense assumed by the United States (more than 6 percent of GNP) and that assumed by Japan (less than 1 percent of GNP). The gap reflects the differing world roles of the two countries, but its size can itself become a source of tension as per capita incomes in the two countries rapidly converge.

As a major economic power without a major military establishment, Japan's position is without historical precedent. How it fulfills its role and responsibility in the world community is a question to which the Japanese people are themselves devoting a great deal of attention and discussion. One way in which Japan can contribute directly to international society is through substantially increasing its economic and technical assistance to low-income countries not only in the traditional areas of Japanese interest in Southeast Asia but in the rest of the developing world as well, including the Indian subcontinent, Africa, and Latin America. Given the domestic and international constraints upon Japan in the military field, a disproportionate participation by Japan in the social and economic development of the low-income countries would be one way for Japan to share the common responsibilities of the world's major economic powers.

No longer can major world economic problems be initially considered within a strictly Atlantic framework, leaving consultation with Japan as something to be carried out at a later stage. If shared responsibilities are to become the basis of Japan's participation in the international economic system, Japan must be a full partner from the beginning of any international discussion of new economic problems and policy directions.

The Japanese View: Economic and Social Problems in the United States

1. Introduction

•••••••••••••••••••••

As the world's largest economic power, the United States has taken a leading role in the accelerated expansion of world trade and the continued development of the world economy since World War II. During the 1960s, however, the relative economic position of the United States steadily declined. This was partly a result of the dramatic rise in the economic capabilities and prospects of the European Community (EC) and Japan and also partly a reflection of growing internal economic difficulties and social tensions.

The combination of the relatively low growth rate of the U.S. economy and inflation has sharpened the problems of unemployment, poverty, and inequitable income distribution. The dominant belief in individualism and the fear of government encroachment upon the rights of individuals and of government intervention in private economic activities have thwarted the development of appropriate public policies on such national problems as industrial adjustment, deteriorating balance of payments, urban decay, and environmental disruption. In addition, U.S. preoccupation with the problems of the cold war and power politics has distorted the allocation of human and physical resources in the direction of the unproductive defense sector and military assistance overseas. This has further aggravated domestic economic and social problems.

97

Recently, however, there have been indications of new developments in both the foreign and domestic policies of the United States. In international relations, as symbolized by the visits of President Nixon to China and the Soviet Union, the United States has begun to seek a new political framework to replace the cold war framework that long characterized its international policies. Domestically, new policies have been implemented that recognize the weaknesses of the market system. These measures would not only supplement the market system but also modify it at the macroeconomic level. These shifts in policy and certain institutional changes appear to be leading the American economy and society slowly but steadily in a new direction.

This study is intended to contribute to a better understanding on our part of the fundamental characteristics of the U.S. economy and the major problems facing it today. Another objective is to trace some of the changes in the basic characteristics, institutions, and policies of the American economy and to present the prospects for the American economy in the 1970s. It is hoped that these analyses of the major problems of the sixties and significant trends of the seventies will form the basis for predicting the likely courses of action to be taken by the United States in formulating a new international economic system in response to changing economic, political, and social conditions.

2. Problems of the 1960s

••••••••••••••••••••••••••••••••••

INFLATION

Until the mid-1960s, the rate of inflation in the United States was, for the most part, quite moderate. Indeed, it was lower than that experienced by other developed countries (see Tables 1 and 2). During the period from 1953 to 1964, price increases were not large; wholesale prices rose at an annual average rate of 0.6 percent, and all consumer prices increased at the rate of 1.3 percent, with 0.7 percent for consumer commodity prices and 2.7 percent for consumer services.

After 1964, however, prices began to rise steadily; and by 1968, the situation became serious. With business activity slowing down, the annual rate of growth of the real gross national product fell from 4.7 percent to 2.7 percent between 1968 and 1969, and in 1970 it fell to –0.5 percent. To deal with the inflation, the government undertook such monetary and fiscal measures as raising the discount rate and restraining fiscal expenditure. The inflation was not contained by these traditional measures, and prices continued to rise; in 1970, the rate of increase in consumer prices reached 5.9 percent.

Rising prices coupled with business slowdown continued into 1971. New economic policies were announced in August 1971 to deal with these problems, and a wage and price freeze was adopted as an anti-inflationary measure. The freeze fixed the upper limit of all prices, rentals, wages, and salaries at the maximum levels that had prevailed during the month prior to August 14, 1971. It was kept in effect for ninety days, until November 13, 1971. For the second phase, the government adopted a policy of legal controls, which allowed price increases only with cost increases and which sought to limit the overall rate of price increases to 2.5 percent annually. The controls limited the annual rate of wage increases to a maximum of 5.5 percent. The wage and price freeze and direct controls were quite effective in bringing about a business recovery and in controlling inflation; the rate of increase of consumer prices fell from more than 5 percent in 1969 and 1970 to 3.2 percent in 1972. Because of the improvement in this situation, the decision to relax direct wage and price controls was made in January 1973, at which point the government instituted the third phase.

From the second half of 1972 on, however, inflationary forces in the United States were strengthened by a new factor, excess demand at home and abroad. For example, a strong domestic demand for wood for home building combined with a strong demand for logs abroad to send timber prices soaring. This raised the average cost of a new home in the United States by $500 in 1972 and by an additional $700 in January 1973 alone. The tendency was further strengthened in 1973, as precipitous price increases accompanied business recovery. The prices of agricultural products, especially such items as beef and wheat, rose sharply, creating economic hardships for the population. Because of this situation, in August 1973, a new sixty-day price freeze was instituted as an emergency anti-inflationary measure. In addition, the government decided to limit exports of soybeans, cottonseed, and other products. Furthermore, in July 1973, as part of the fourth phase, the federal government announced new control measures that limited price increases to the amount of cost increases. These measures were not successful in controlling inflation.

BALANCE OF PAYMENTS

The U.S. balance of payments has been in deficit nearly every year since 1950. Three persistent patterns were seen in the U.S. balance-of-payments situation until the mid-sixties: (1) a large surplus in the trade balance, (2) a deficit in the transfer balance because of governmental economic and military aid, and (3) a conspicuous outflow of private capi-

Table 1. ANNUAL CHANGES IN WHOLESALE AND CONSUMER PRICES IN THE UNITED STATES, 1950–1971 *(percent)*

	WHOLESALE PRICES			CONSUMER PRICES		
	All com-modities	Farm products and food	Industrial	All items	Com-modities	Services
1950	3.9	4.8	3.6	1.0	0.6	3.2
1951	11.4	13.8	10.4	7.9	9.0	5.3
1952	−2.7	−3.9	−2.3	2.2	1.3	4.4
1953	−1.4	−6.5	0.8	0.8	−0.3	4.3
1954	0.2	−0.3	0.2	0.5	−0.9	3.3
1955	0.2	−4.7	2.2	−0.4	−0.9	2.0
1956	3.3	−0.7	4.5	1.5	0.9	2.5
1957	2.9	3.4	2.8	3.6	3.1	4.0
1958	1.4	4.7	0.3	2.7	2.3	3.8
1959	0.2	−4.7	1.8	0.8	0.1	2.9
1960	0.1	0.2	—	1.6	0.9	3.3
1961	−0.4	—	−0.5	1.0	0.5	2.0
1962	0.3	1.1	—	1.1	0.9	1.9
1963	−0.3	−1.0	−0.1	1.2	0.9	2.0
1964	0.2	−0.6	0.5	1.3	1.1	1.9
1965	2.0	4.2	1.3	1.7	1.2	2.2
1966	3.3	6.6	2.2	2.9	2.6	3.9
1967	0.2	−3.4	1.5	2.9	1.8	4.4
1968	2.5	2.4	2.5	4.2	3.7	5.2
1969	3.9	5.5	3.4	5.4	4.5	6.9
1970	3.7	3.3	3.8	5.9	4.7	8.1
1971	3.2	2.0	3.6	4.3	3.4	5.6

Source: U.S. Bureau of the Census, *Statistical Abstract of the United States: 1972.*

tal in the capital account. Basic changes have occurred in the first and third patterns since the late sixties. A deficit in the trade balance has appeared since 1971, the first time in the postwar period. The capital account also showed a deficit. In the late sixties, the inflow of investment income, which had increased steadily during the decade, surpassed the outflow, which continued on a large scale.

Placing this economic transition within its historical context, we can see that the Korean War marked the shift in American foreign policy from economic aid for post–World War II recovery to direct military spending and military aid in Europe. Moreover, with the economic recovery in Europe, American private capital began to flow rapidly into European countries in the early fifties; it increased from more than $1 billion to more than $3 billion in the latter half of the fifties. The U.S. trade balance during that decade consistently showed a large surplus (see Table 3).

During the first half of the sixties, the trade surplus was even greater than that during the fifties. In the capital account, the expansion of the European regional market precipitated by the European Community treaty of 1958 accelerated the outflow of U.S. private capital. However, the increasing deficits in the balance of payments since the late fifties have caused a decrease in gold holdings; and after 1961, several measures were taken to deal with the resulting loss of confidence in the U.S. dollar. Among the measures were efforts to promote productivity growth, to stimulate "buy American" sentiments, to expand exports, and to reduce imports. Furthermore, voluntary restraint on the part of American private enterprises with regard to their foreign investments and loans was encouraged.

In the latter half of the 1960s, the pattern of the balance of payments that had characterized the postwar period began to change. From 1965 on, the size of the trade surplus began to shrink, falling as low as $624 million in 1968, or one-tenth the $6.8 billion surplus of 1964. This tendency continued until 1971, when the trade balance reached a deficit figure.

The outflow of both short-term and long-term private capital grew consistently in the 1960s, reaching $6.8 billion in 1970 and $8.7 billion in 1971. On the other hand, the annual inflow of investment income increased from over $3 billion in 1960 to more than $6 billion in the second half of the 1960s, continuously surpassing the annual outflow of private capital. Income from foreign investments reached $4.1 billion in 1969 and, after dropping to $3.5 billion in 1970, peaked again at $4.7 billion in 1971. Thus, income earned on long-term investments abroad has in recent years been the major contributor to the U.S. balance of payments.

Table 2. ANNUAL CHANGE IN WHOLESALE AND CONSUMER PRICES IN MAJOR DEVELOPED COUNTRIES, 1963–1972 *(percent)*

	WHOLESALE PRICES					
	United States	Japan	United Kingdom	West Germany	France	Italy
1963	−0.3	1.7	1.1	0.5	3.2	5.2
1964	0.2	0.2	2.9	1.1	2.1	3.3
1965	2.0	0.8	3.8	2.4	1.2	1.7
1966	3.3	2.4	2.6	1.7	2.5	1.5
1967	0.2	1.9	1.2	−0.9	−0.6	−0.2
1968	2.5	0.8	4.0	4.0	0.6	0.4
1969	3.9	2.2	3.9	2.7	9.4	3.9
1970	3.7	3.6	6.6	6.0	7.3	7.3
1971	3.2	−0.8	7.8	4.6	3.7	3.4
1972	4.6	0.8	5.3	3.1	5.8	4.1
Average annual change	2.3	1.4	3.9	2.5	3.5	3.0

	CONSUMER PRICES					
	United States	Japan	United Kingdom	West Germany	France	Italy
1963	1.2	7.6	2.0	2.9	4.8	7.6
1964	1.3	3.8	3.3	2.4	3.4	5.9
1965	1.7	7.6	4.8	3.1	2.5	4.5
1966	2.9	5.1	3.9	3.7	2.7	2.4
1967	2.9	3.9	2.5	1.7	2.7	3.7
1968	4.2	5.3	4.7	1.6	4.5	1.4
1969	5.4	5.5	5.4	2.7	6.4	2.7
1970	5.9	7.9	6.4	3.8	5.2	4.9
1971	4.3	6.2	9.4	5.2	5.5	4.8
1972	3.2	4.6	7.1	5.8	6.2	5.7
Average annual change	3.3	5.7	4.9	3.3	4.4	4.3

Source: Bank of Japan, *Japan and the World* (1972).

Table 3. U.S. BALANCE OF PAYMENTS, 1946–1972 *(millions of dolla*

	1946–1949	1950–1954	1955–1959	1960	1961	1962
Trade balance	27,868	10,813	18,531	4,906	5,588	4,56
Military transaction, net	−1,543	3,296	−2,437	−987	−1,131	−91
Balance on services	6,660	8,526	10,604	1,981	2,629	3,03
Balance on transfers	−16,540	−26,903	−23,908	−4,025	−3,951	−4,15
Balance on capital flows	−12,710	−5,167	−14,056	−4,618	−4,404	−3,49
U.S. private capital flows	−2,859	−5,478	−13,214	−3,878	−4,180	−3,42
Errors and omissions, net	2,848	1,007	2,394	−1,156	−1,103	−1,24
Net liquidity balance	6,583	−8,428	−8,872	−3,901	−2,371	−2,20

Source: U.S. Department of Commerce, *Survey of Current Business* (various issues).

UNEMPLOYMENT

The United States traditionally has tolerated a much higher level of unemployment than have most other developed countries (see Table 4). For example, the unemployment rates in West Germany and Japan have generally been in the range of 1 to 2 percent; whereas that of the United States has always been higher, above 3 percent. Even the full-scale intervention in the Vietnam War in 1966 did not cause the rate to fall below 3 percent, and since then, it has ranged between 4 and 6 percent because of cyclical fluctuations. The Nixon administration set 4.5 percent as the target for the end of 1973.

The range within which unemployment fluctuates is wider in the United States than it is in other developed countries. The unemployment rate in the United States tends to be more than 2 percent higher in periods of recession than in periods of prosperity.

Tables 5 and 6 indicate some of the structural characteristics of unemployment in the United States. Unemployment rates are higher among blacks, women, and youth than among other segments of the labor force. Although the unemployment rate among blacks has shown some improve-

104

1963	1964	1965	1966	1967	1968	1969	1970	1971	1972
5,241	6,831	4,951	3,926	3,860	624	638	2,110	−2,689	−6,816
−742	−793	−494	−1,933	−2,233	−2,336	−2,576	−2,758	−2,894	−3,541
3,045	3,881	4,292	4,829	4,492	5,014	4,648	4,851	6,309	6,137
−4,277	−4,037	−4,326	−3,810	−3,874	−3,632	−3,594	−3,761	−3,575	−3,764
−5,430	−7,565	−5,121	−3,312	−4,714	1,021	−3,412	−4,032	−8,843	−2,894
−4,459	−6,578	−3,794	−4,310	−5,655	−5,412	−5,374	−6,886	−8,710	—
−509	−1,118	−576	−489	−1,007	−514	−2,924	−1,132	−10,314	−3,096
−2,670	−2,800	−1,335	−1,357	−3,544	171	−7,221	−4,720	−22,006	−13,974

ment, it remains twice as high as the rate among whites. Unemployment rates are also much higher in certain depressed regions of the country than they are for the nation as a whole. These characteristics indicate that the unemployment problem in the United States cannot be solved with easier money and spending policies alone, for the problem originates largely from the American economic and social structure.

Official levels of unemployment understate actual unemployment. According to the official definition of unemployment, people are counted as unemployed only if they are actively seeking employment. Therefore, people who become discouraged by the lack of job opportunities and cease to seek work actively are not counted. The number of such people is large, particularly during periods of recession.

POVERTY AND INEQUALITY

National income per capita in the United States was $4,477 in 1972. This was the highest figure in the world and accounts for the country being considered the wealthiest in the world. However, even in this country, there are serious and unique problems concerning poverty and inequality in income distribution.

The Social Security Administration's 1970 definition of poverty was an income of less than $3,968 for an urban family of four. In that year, according to the same criteria, some 25.5 million Americans, or 12.6 percent of the population, were living below the poverty level. Changes between 1959 and 1970 in the absolute number and proportion of the poor, by racial group, according to this definition appear in Table 7. As the table shows, in 1970, 9.9 percent of whites and 32.1 percent of blacks were below the poverty level. The poor are concentrated among certain groups, such as blacks, and in certain geographic regions.

Moreover, in the United States, there is a tendency for goods with low income elasticity of demand to have higher prices. This is reflected in the relatively high costs of such essential services as education, medical care, and public transportation. This affects people in the lowest income classes unfavorably, forcing them either to bear a heavy financial burden or to accept lower-quality benefits.

In order to solve the problems of poverty in any fundamental way, improvement of education is absolutely necessary; children from low-income families must be given the opportunity to receive high-quality education. However, in the United States, considerable authority is vested in local governments, and control of primary and secondary educational institutions is dispersed among about 25,000 school districts. The share of the educational costs that local governments must bear is high; federal and state governments pay 50 percent of such costs, and local governments pay 50 percent. In Japan, by contrast, the national and prefectural governments pay 80 percent, whereas local governments pay 20 percent. Furthermore, since the revenues of local governments depend heavily upon the property tax, there are large differences in educational quality from area to area, depending upon the wealth of the area. In metropolitan regions, where the phenomenon of residential polarization exists, narrowing these differences becomes a great task for local governments.

POLLUTION

The problem of pollution is common to all highly industrialized countries. In Japan, it has become an especially urgent problem because of space and other physical limitations, and it may therefore appear that solutions to pollution problems are more readily available in the United

Table 4. UNEMPLOYMENT RATE IN MAJOR DEVELOPED COUNTRIES, 1955–1972 *(percent)*

	United States	Japan	United Kingdom	West Germany	Italy
1955	4.4	2.5	1.1	5.1	9.8
1960	5.5	1.7	1.6	1.3	4.2
1965	4.5	1.2	1.4	0.7	3.6
1967	3.8	1.3	2.2	2.1	3.5
1968	3.6	1.2	2.4	1.5	3.5
1969	3.5	1.1	2.4	0.9	3.4
1970	4.9	1.2	2.5	0.7	3.1
1971	5.9	1.2	3.3	0.9	3.1
1972	5.6	1.4	3.7	1.1	—

Source: Bank of Japan, *Quarterly Bulletin of Foreign Economic Statistics* (March 1973).

Table 5. UNEMPLOYMENT RATES IN THE UNITED STATES, BY SEX AND RACE, 1960–1972 *(percent)*

	1960	1965	1967	1968	1969	1970	1971	1972
All workers	5.5	4.5	3.8	3.6	3.5	4.9	5.9	5.6
White	4.9	4.1	3.4	3.2	3.1	4.5	5.4	5.0
Male	4.8	3.6	2.7	2.6	2.5	4.0	4.9	4.5
Female	5.3	5.0	4.6	4.3	4.2	5.4	6.3	5.9
Black and other	10.2	8.1	7.4	6.7	6.4	8.2	9.9	10.0
Male	10.7	7.4	6.0	5.6	5.3	7.3	9.1	8.9
Female	9.4	9.2	9.1	8.3	7.8	9.3	10.8	11.3
Ratio of black and other to white	2.1	2.0	2.2	2.1	2.1	1.8	1.8	2.0

Sources: U.S. Bureau of the Census, *Statistical Abstract of the United States: 1972*; and *Manpower Report of the President — March 1973.*

States than in Japan. Pollution in the United States, however, has its own characteristics, which make solutions to problems difficult to find.

According to a 1966 study conducted by the National Academy of Sciences, if the accelerating rate at which organic wastes are discharged into American surface waters is maintained, then the oxygen absorbed through the decomposition of the waste would use up the total oxygen content of surface waters by the year 2000. That is, in twenty-seven years, surface waters would be incapable of self-purification or of supporting any form of life. Many bodies of water are approaching this condition at a rate much faster than the average. Lake Erie is perhaps the most prominent example, but the serious pollution of waterways is a national problem.

The problem of air pollution is equally serious. Photochemical smog now blankets nearly every major city in the United States and many smaller ones as well. The emissions of such polluting substances as carbon monoxide and hydrocarbons reached 208 million tons in 1970. As Table 8 indicates, more than 50 percent of this total is from transportation, mainly automobiles. Automobile-generated pollution, particularly in major cities, is alarming, affecting the human body directly or through photochemical smog. To improve this situation, stringent standards for regulating automobile exhaust emissions were set by the 1970 amendment to the Clean Air Act and were scheduled to become effective in 1975; but in 1973, at the request of the automobile industry, enforcement of the act was postponed for one year.

Solid wastes, in addition to being ugly, also cause air pollution when disposed of. However, as long as the economic philosophy, institutions, and policy of mass production, mass consumption, and mass disposal continue, the situation will continue to worsen. In the United States, this problem is particularly serious in terms of the automobile (see Table 9). Besides pollutants from the burning of fuel, substances such as agricultural chemicals and detergents have become sources of serious pollution problems.

URBAN PROBLEMS

Problems caused by the concentration of population in urban areas are common to all developed countries, although the problems vary in their seriousness from country to country. In the United States, because of the existence of racial problems and the widespread use of automobiles, urban problems tend to be quite serious and to contain unique American characteristics. The following urban problems can be considered among

Table 6. UNEMPLOYMENT RATES IN THE UNITED STATES, BY RACE AND REGION, 1971 *(percent)*

REGION	TOTAL	MINORITY RACES
United States	5.9	9.9
Northeast	6.2	9.3
New England	6.9	16.2
Middle Atlantic	6.0	8.5
North Central	5.5	12.8
East North Central	6.0	13.3
West North Central	4.3	10.4
South	4.9	8.8
South Atlantic	4.5	7.4
East South Central	5.2	10.1
West South Central	5.3	11.0
West	8.1	10.7
Mountain	6.1	11.5
Pacific	8.7	10.6

Source: U.S. Bureau of the Census, *Statistical Abstract of the United States: 1972.*

Table 7. PERSONS BELOW THE POVERTY LEVEL IN THE UNITED STATES, BY RACE, 1959–1971 *(percent of population)*

	1959	1963	1965	1967	1968	1969	1970	1971
All persons	22.4	19.5	17.3	14.2	12.8	12.2	12.6	12.5
White	18.1	15.3	13.3	11.0	10.0	9.5	9.9	9.9
Black and other	56.2	51.0	47.1	37.2	33.5	31.1	32.1	30.9

Source: U.S. Bureau of the Census, *Current Population Reports*, P-60, No. 86, "Characteristics of the Low-Income Population, 1971," Table 1.

Table 8. MAJOR AIR POLLUTANT EMISSIONS IN THE UNITED STATES, 1971 (*millions of tons*)

	Carbon monoxide	Sulfur oxides	Partic-ulates	Hydro-carbons	Nitrogen oxides	Total
Transportation	77.5	1.0	1.0	14.7	11.2	105.4
Stationary fuel combustion	1.0	26.3	6.5	0.3	10.2	44.3
Industrial processes	11.4	5.1	13.6	5.6	0.2	35.9
Refuse disposal	3.8	0.1	0.7	1.0	0.2	5.8
Miscellaneous	6.5	0.1	5.2	5.0	0.2	17.0
Total	100.2	32.6	27.0	26.6	22.0	208.4

Source: U.S. Council on Environmental Quality, *Environmental Quality: The Fourth Annual Report* (Washington, D.C.: U.S. Government Printing Office, 1973).

Table 9. SCRAPPAGE RATE OF AUTOMOBILES IN MAJOR DEVELOPED COUNTRIES (*percent*)

	United States	Japan	West Germany	France	Italy
1960	66.1	4.6	15.0	19.6	16.8
1965	64.9	13.2	32.0	22.7	10.0
1970	64.1	22.4	42.7	38.3	24.1

Note: Scrappage rate equals that percent of new-car registrations required to replace the cars scrapped.
Source: Japan Automobile Manufacturers Association.

Table 10. CRIMES KNOWN TO THE POLICE, BY TYPE AND
AREA, IN THE UNITED STATES, 1971

(rate per 100,000 inhabitants)

	SMSAs[a]		Other Cities		Rural Areas	
	Total	*Rate*	*Total*	*Rate*	*Total*	*Rate*
Property crimes	4,458,000	3,056	392,000	1,698	335,000	899
Violent crimes	716,000	491	45,000	193	50,000	133
Total	5,174,000	3,547	436,000	1,891	385,000	1,032

[a] Standard Metropolitan Statistical Area.
Source: U.S. Bureau of the Census, *Statistical Abstract of the United States: 1972.*

the most significant: crime, residential polarization, housing, education, pollution, transportation.

Crime. The crime rate in the United States has increased three times in the last decade. Moreover, crime rates in the largest cities are twice as high as those in smaller ones and 3.5 times as high as those of nonurban areas (see Table 10).

Residential polarization. In the decade between 1960 and 1970, population in the central areas of the cities grew at the rate of 4 percent among whites and 39 percent among blacks (see Table 11). As the black population in the central parts of cities has increased, a large number of white middle-class people have simultaneously moved into the suburbs. Although many middle-class people do live in the cities, one phenomenon that has occurred is polarization, with the rich living in well-secured luxury apartments and the poor living in the ghettos.

Housing. High real estate prices, land taxes, and construction costs have also contributed to residential polarization in the cities. Renovation and maintenance are extremely expensive and have increased in cost

111

Table 11. U.S. POPULATION, BY AREA AND RACE, 1950–1970

	Population (thousands)			Rate of Increase from Previous Census (percent)		
	Total	White	Black and other	Total	White	Black and other
1950, total population	151,326	135,150	16,176	—	—	—
Urban	96,847	86,864	9,983	—	—	—
Inside urbanized areas	69,249	61,925	7,324	—	—	—
Central cities	48,377	42,042	6,335	—	—	—
Urban fringe	20,872	19,883	989	—	—	—
Outside urbanized areas	27,598	24,939	2,659	—	—	—
Rural	54,479	48,286	6,193	—	—	—
1960, total population	179,323	158,832	20,491	18.5	8.5	26.7
Urban	125,269	110,428	14,840	29.3	27.1	48.7
Inside urbanized areas	95,848	83,770	12,079	38.4	35.3	64.9
Central cities	57,975	47,627	10,348	19.8	13.3	63.3
Urban fringe	37,873	36,143	1,731	81.5	81.8	75.0
Outside urbanized areas	29,420	26,658	2,762	6.6	6.9	3.9
Rural	54,054	48,403	5,651	−0.01	0.02	−0.9
1970, total population	203,212	177,749	25,463	13.3	11.9	24.3
Urban	149,325	128,773	20,552	19.2	16.6	38.5
Inside urbanized areas	118,447	100,952	17,495	23.6	20.5	44.8
Central cities	63,922	49,547	14,375	10.3	4.0	38.9
Urban fringe	54,525	51,405	3,120	44.0	42.2	80.2
Outside urbanized areas	30,878	27,822	3,057	5.0	4.4	10.7
Rural	53,887	48,976	4,911	−0.03	1.2	−13.1

Source: U.S. Bureau of the Census, *Statistical Abstract of the United States: 1972.*

much faster than the ability of low-income families to pay for them. In many cases, deteriorated housing could be made ·into attractive residences; but few ghetto dwellers can afford to do so, and overall neighborhood, deterioration makes such action unattractive for those who can. The problems of the ghetto, however, are part of large social problems that are beyond the power of the individual to remedy.

Education. Raising educational standards among blacks and others living in poverty is indispensable to a basic solution of urban problems and is closely related to the problem of unequal income distribution.

Pollution. The problem of waste disposal is growing exponentially, potential costs are increasing correspondingly, and the technology for suitable disposal remains to be developed. Air pollution, largely but by no means exclusively automobile-generated, is a particular problem in urban and metropolitan areas.

Transportation. American cities have been shaped and choked by the automobile while mass transit facilities have been allowed to decay or remain undeveloped. The decay and deterioration of public transportation facilities have caused great hardship to the lower-income classes, who must depend upon them. Furthermore, the increase in automobile use has caused traffic congestion, air pollution, and other problems. Locational patterns based on automobile traffic, however, will be difficult to alter.

3. Underlying Economic and Social Factors

● ●

A SURVEY OF THE MAJOR ECONOMIC AND SOCIAL PROBLEMS facing the United States today suggests that many of these problems are closely linked and are caused by common factors, which in turn are fundamental to the basic institutions and structure of the economy. Although all these economic and social problems have been recognized by the successive administrations during the postwar period, the preoccupation with maintaining the U.S. leadership position in world politics and military affairs has prevented the government from initiating those public policies necessary for coping with the problems.

INFLATION

There has been much debate on the causes of the stubborn inflation that has troubled the United States since the mid-sixties. Most observers agree that the extraordinary expansion in the military outlays in conjunction with the escalated war in Vietnam beginning in 1965 was responsible for sharp rises in both wholesale and consumer prices. Others have stressed the emergence of excess aggregate demand at home and abroad. At home, this demand was generated by the Johnson administration's policy of guns and butter inaugurated even before 1965. Abroad, it was caused partly by the increased international liquidity resulting from the continuing deterioration in the U.S. balance of payments and partly by the full-employment policies pursued in almost all the developed countries, which led to worldwide inflation. The fixed exchange rate system under the International Monetary Fund (IMF) agreement increased the impact of inflation abroad, and the recent devaluation of the dollar raised the prices of imports still higher. Still other observers have attributed the persistence of inflation to the monopolistic power of trade unions and the oligopolistic structure of major markets that generate upward pressures in wages and prices. It is believed that in recent years, the rising concern with the environment has brought growing constraints on output expansion in the United States, thus contributing to a more rapid rise in prices of many essential commodities in reaction to a rising demand for them.

The Vietnam War was unpopular both domestically and abroad, and large-scale involvement in it in the mid-sixties coincided with essentially full employment at home. The war could have been financed in a noninflationary way through an increase in taxes or through the sacrifice of domestic programs inaugurated by the Johnson administration under the banner of the Great Society. Neither course would have been popular or feasible; attempts would have intensified public and political pressures for the United States to reduce its involvement in Vietnam.

The extent of the monopolistic and political power possessed by different groups of workers, of which construction workers, doctors, printers, and electricians provide prime examples, has served as a model for others. A mood of increased militancy prevailed in many major trade unions from the mid-sixties and resulted in large wage gains for teamsters, public transport workers, and others. The civil rights and antiwar movements also influenced the increased militancy of many labor groups formerly victimized by their own respectability or lack of organization.

In each case of increased labor militancy, a significant share of the increased wages was passed on to the public in the form of higher prices, charges, taxes, or public fees; thus a vicious cycle set in. The consequence is so-called aggression inflation: Various groups, business as well as labor, seek to increase their own share of the national income, and the total claim is greater than that income at current prices.

In this context, depressing aggregate demand through conventional fiscal and monetary policies would achieve little more than adding to unemployment. The recession of 1970–1971 was the result of just such policies, and it would have had to be much deeper and more prolonged to have cured the inflationary virus. Turning a moderate recession into a deep depression, however, would have been clearly unacceptable. In this context, the decision was made to impose wage and price controls.

From 1972 on, however, inflationary forces in the United States have been strengthened by a new factor, excess demand at home and abroad. For example, a strong domestic and foreign demand for foodstuffs, industrial raw materials, and fuels, precipitated by either short-run reduced supplies (as in foodstuffs) or long-term monopolistic price increases (as in petroleum), has generated the climate of worldwide inflation, pushing domestic prices still higher for many basic commodities. The devaluation of the U.S. dollar in December 1971 and again in February 1973 amplified the impact of inflation upon the general level of prices in the United States. A similar problem exists in the agricultural sector, in which steep price increases over the past year almost completely undercut the Nixon administration's efforts to limit price rises in 1973.

The negative impact of inflation on social welfare will produce popular support for anti-inflationary measures, and government efforts as shown in its four phases of wage and price controls will intensify. However, because many of the causes of inflation are structural and deeply imbedded in the basic institutions and structure of the economy, success in the battle against inflation will probably be limited. To bring the current spiraling inflation to a halt requires structural remedies in the labor and product markets and changes in both the national decision-making process and the concept of the role of the federal government in the national economy. Reforms are also required in the international monetary system as well as increased cooperation and coordination in monetary and fiscal policies among major nations.

BALANCE-OF-PAYMENTS DETERIORATION

Many of the factors causing inflation have also been responsible for the deterioration in the American balance of payments that has continued since the mid-fifties. Of the major factors that have contributed to worsening the U.S. balance-of-payments position over the decade, the following are the most significant: the huge amount of military and economic aid overseas, particularly after the expansion of U.S. involvement in the Vietnam War in the mid-sixties; the steady expansion of the U.S. demand for imports associated with the domestic inflation and the rising level of personal income and expenditures coupled with the decline in American competition in overseas markets; and the spread of the U.S. capital invest-

Table 12. ENROLLMENTS IN INSTITUTIONS OF
           HIGHER EDUCATION,
           SELECTED DEVELOPED COUNTRIES,
           SELECTED YEARS *(per 1,000 inhabitants)*

	Year	Enrollment
Japan	1969	16.2
United States	1968	34.7
United Kingdom	1967	6.2
France	1967	10.6
West Germany	1967	5.8
Soviet Union	1968	18.9

Source: Japan. Ministry of Education, *White Paper on Education*, 1970.

Table 13. EXPENDITURES AND MANPOWER FOR
           RESEARCH AND DEVELOPMENT,
           SELECTED DEVELOPED COUNTRIES, 1963

	Expenditures as Percent of GNP	Number of Research Workers (thousands)	Ratio of Research Workers per 1,000 Inhabitants
Belgium	0.89	7.6	0.82
France	1.58	31.8	0.67
West Germany	1.81	37.7	0.69
Italy	0.64	17.9	0.35
Japan	1.30	115.0	1.20
United Kingdom	2.28	58.7	1.10
United States	2.89	436.0	2.30

Source: UNESCO, *Technological Development in Japan* (1971).

ment abroad, spearheaded by U.S.-based multinational corporations and aided by the fixed exchange rate system based on the overvalued U.S. dollar. The persistence of international monetary crises against the huge and rapidly rising U.S. dollar overhang abroad, which at times results in an upsurge in the outflow of short-term capital from the United States, has also compounded the deterioration in U.S. balance of payments. The long-run trend toward declining rates of productivity improvement associated with the changing structure of the U.S. economy points to the greater expansion of the service rather than of the manufacturing sector. Set against the background of steadily rising wages and prices in general, this has contributed greatly to the equally long-run trend toward deteriorating U.S. balance of payments. This has encouraged U.S. imports and capital investment overseas and discouraged U.S. exports, particularly of domestic manufactures of comparatively high labor intensity.

In historical perspective, the "fall" of the U.S. dollar (seen in the devaluation moves) from its preeminent position in the international monetary system must be understood as part of the long-run economic decline of the United States relative to other countries in the world. The basic force behind this decline and the monetary instability it has brought with it has been the slow growth in productivity in the U.S. economy. The United States has been the world leader in higher education (see Table 12). It has had faster population growth and invested larger amounts of money and human resources in research and development than most other developed countries (see Table 13). Furthermore, one might be led to expect that the much higher level of per capita income in the United States would facilitate savings and that the large, oligopolistic firms would be suitable vehicles for accelerated investment. Yet the United States has distinctly lagged behind the world's principal industrial countries in terms of growth of productivity (see Table 14).

Several factors are responsible for this slow growth in productivity, but the single most important one is associated with the lack of the organizational imperatives of modern technology in the United States. These appear in other developed countries in the form of indicative planning, close collaboration between the public and private sectors, and various kinds of far-reaching collaboration within the private sector itself. What these forms provide above all is the assurance that necessary complementary investments and government support will be forthcoming.

In the United States, the barriers to appropriate public measures to stimulate growth and productivity improvement via institutional change

Table 14. INDEXES OF OUTPUT PER MAN-HOUR IN MANUFACTURING, SELECTED DEVELOPED COUNTRIES, 1960–1969 (1960=100)

	1961	1962	1963	1964	1965	1966	1967	1968	1969
United States	102.4	108.1	112.5	117.9	122.6	124.1	124.2	130.1	132.8
Belgium	102.2	109.9	115.0	123.2	128.2	137.3	147.5	159.4	169.5
Canada	104.5	112.1	116.3	121.2	125.6	129.0	131.4	139.3	144.7
France	104.4	109.1	113.7	119.5	126.3	133.9	141.6	150.3	167.0
West Germany	105.7	112.5	118.6	127.6	137.0	142.0	151.1	161.5	168.0
Italy	103.7	113.8	117.5	125.3	140.9	147.5	153.6	165.9	167.9
Japan	113.3	118.1	127.8	144.7	150.2	166.0	190.1	218.3	251.0
Netherlands	104.9	108.0	112.3	122.6	128.4	136.0	145.1	160.2	176.8
Sweden[a]	104.0	111.0	118.4	131.2	140.6	148.5	160.0	177.4	191.4
United Kingdom	101.1	103.0	107.9	114.7	118.2	121.7	125.3	133.0	135.8

Source: U. S. Bureau of the Census, *Statistical Abstract of the United States: 1971.*

[a]Includes mining.

are to be found in the nation's historical experience and ideology. Free competition and laissez-faire were found to be congenial to efforts for industrialization in the nineteenth century. These doctrines, buttressed by the value Americans place on individualism, have evolved into a deep suspicion of public leadership in the economy, of public-private collaboration, and of collaboration within the private sector. Thus, just at a time when technological development has made such organizational changes necessary in order to accelerate economic growth and productivity improvement, the United States has been unable to initiate them or to grasp their significance fully.

The role that the slow growth in the productivity rate has played in the deterioration of the U.S. balance of payments must be understood in relation to inflation, to short-term capital flows, and to international liquidity, with which these two other factors are associated. The basic institutional constraint created by the adjustable-peg system under the IMF agreement increased the impact of the various factors working to produce steady deterioration in the U.S. balance-of-payments position. With the floating rate system now in operation and worldwide inflation rampant among the major developed countries, the United States has a better chance of improving its balance-of-payments position, as is indicated by experience in recent months. Basically, however, unless the nation succeeds in increasing the growth in the productivity rate and in further restraining inflationary forces, ever-increasing worldwide liquidity will precipitate international monetary crises and possibly have an even more negative effect on the U.S. balance-of-payments position.

The future direction of the movement of U.S. balance of payments also depends on the speed with which the United States changes its foreign policy objectives. Historically, the United States has maintained a surplus in the balance of trade—a surplus that has been instrumental in financing the costs of pursuing its foreign policy objectives. If no shift in foreign policy emphasis takes place, U.S. foreign policy costs will continue to exert a considerable drain on the U.S. balance of payments, a drain that will have to be offset by improvements in the trade and investment balances.

PERSISTENT HIGH UNEMPLOYMENT

The persistence of high rates of unemployment in the American economy has been ascribed to various causes, including: a relatively slow growth of the total output of goods and services compared with a steady increase in the size of the labor force; reduced rates of productivity increases; long-term practices that allow management to resort easily to layoffs in time of recession; the influence of trade unions that have tended to place higher priority on the size of annual wage increments than on employment security and new job creation; racial discrimination in industry and in the trade union movement; the spread of multinational corporations overseas; and very significantly, the lack of appropriate manpower policies at the federal, state, and local government levels.

Traditional U.S. toleration of a high level of unemployment reflects a lack of public initiative, since much unemployment derives from structural causes and can be alleviated only by measures designed to influence social institutions and organizations. It reflects, too, the misapplication of the values of individualism and individual responsibility to circumstances that the individual does not have the power to remedy.

Manpower policies at the federal level were first instituted by the Kennedy administration in the Area Redevelopment Act of 1961 and the Manpower Development and Training Act of 1962. These pieces of legislation were intended to alleviate conditions in depressed areas and to offer opportunities for workers suffering from prolonged unemployment. The Trade Expansion Act of 1962 had similar provisions for workers displaced through increased imports from abroad; it extended adjustment assistance to such workers as well as to companies affected under liberalized trade. These federal laws, however, were limited in their objectives and coverage and did not apply to the overall need to upgrade the education and skills of American workers regardless of their current employment status or personal predicament. In this sense, the United States failed to put forth comprehensive government planning and initiatives in manpower development and specifically that of blacks, women, and youth, segments of the population with the greatest need for such programs.

A high level of unemployment is typical of the U.S. economy in general, but unemployment rates have been traditionally much higher among blacks, women, and youth than among white adult male workers. Aside from differences in the quality of the labor force of each of these groups, the institutional setup that works against the former group of workers has been mainly responsible for their unemployment. The American system of layoffs is based on seniority. Workers who have the least seniority, and therefore tend to be least skilled and experienced, are laid off first. Workers with longer service thus have better protection than workers with shorter service, who tend to be blacks, women, or youth. Cyclical downturns in business cause huge increases in the number of the unemployed among blacks, women, and youth. They fall into the pool of long-duration unemployed and thus are structurally unemployed. The layoff system also brings about interrupted employment, which retards manpower development and skill formation and thus is costly to the national economy as a whole.

Direct investment overseas by U.S. corporations, particularly by multinational corporations with production facilities abroad, has been singled out by the American trade union movement as causing the export of American jobs. Although in some specific instances American jobs have been lost as a result of direct U.S. investment overseas, the evidence is not as clear as unions have claimed it to be. According to a recent study by the U.S. Tariff Commission, "some American industries with heavy overseas investment have contributed most to U.S. exports and have had the least impact on the upsurge of U.S. imports." This suggests that U.S.-based multinational corporations have in fact created jobs for American workers.

Solutions to problems of structural unemployment will require institutional reforms and specific policy measures that might shake the foundations of American management, the trade union movement, and business-government relationships. In spite of an increased recognition of the need for specific measures, a strategy for dealing with structural unemployment remains to be devised and implemented.

INEQUALITY IN INCOME DISTRIBUTION

According to the definition prepared by the U.S. Department of Labor's Bureau of Labor Statistics (BLS), about 20 percent of four-person families were living in poverty in the United States in 1969. Furthermore, 2.5 million families in which both the husband and the wife are wage earners depend on the wife's earnings for over one-half the family income. In many cases, the woman's income is crucial in moving the family from poverty to middle-class comfort. Without the increased participation of female workers in the labor force, poverty in America would be far more serious and greater in magnitude.

Although a modest trend toward greater equality in income distribution appears to exist, this is accounted for almost entirely by the exclusion of capital gains from Bureau of the Census estimates (see Table 15). Federal income taxes have little influence on the distribution of after-tax income. Since property and sales taxes, both highly regressive, are the principal forms of revenue for state and local governments, the distribu-

Table 15. DISTRIBUTION OF BEFORE-TAX FAMILY INCOME IN THE UNITED STATES, 1947–1969
(percent)

	1947	1950	1956	1960	1964	1969
Poorest fifth	5.0	4.5	5.0	4.9	5.2	5.6
Second fifth	11.8	12.0	12.4	12.0	12.0	12.3
Middle fifth	17.0	17.4	17.8	17.6	17.7	17.6
Fourth fifth	23.1	23.5	23.7	23.6	24.0	23.4
Richest fifth	43.0	42.6	41.2	42.0	41.1	41.0
Richest 5 percent	17.2	17.0	16.3	16.8	15.7	14.7

Source: Richard Edwards et al., *The Capitalist System* (Englewood Cliffs, N.J.: Prentice-Hall, 1972).

tion of disposable income after such nonfederal taxes is highly unequal. State and local taxes thus tend to offset the modestly progressive impact of federal taxation. Furthermore, the distribution of disposable income would be much more unequal than that of gross income because the prices of essential consumer goods and services tend to rise faster than those of nonessential commodities.

Ideological barriers in the United States against drastic public measures act to maintain the persistent inequality in income distribution. Part of the ideological reasoning is that unequal rewards provide the basis for labor motivation and that unequal distribution of income and wealth is more conducive to capital accumulation, since the marginal propensity to save would be higher among the higher-income group than among the lower-income one. Many factors militate against the solution of the problems of poverty and inequality in the United States, but one in particular might be noted here. Under circumstances in which wants and needs are always being created that capture the rich as well as the poor, it would be difficult to encourage people who are better off to forgo consumption via taxation and the transfer of money to those with greater need. Instead, income differentials are perceived in terms of the worthiness of the affluent and the personal inadequacy of the poor, a view in line with the American belief in individualism. On these grounds, unemployment insurance and other social security programs were long opposed until their enactment in the early thirties, just as welfare programs have been and still are opposed. President Nixon's position against expanded welfare program expenditures was revealed in the federal budget for fiscal 1973 and was also based on this traditional American belief.

Poverty and inequality do not relate solely to the issue of race relations in the United States; however, no discussion of these problems can ignore their racial overtones. Inequality in income among the races reflects differences in education, skills, work experiences, employment and promotion opportunities, and trade union membership. Although these are difficult differences to overcome, in recent years greater attention has been being given to the need to improve equality in income distribution.

Problems of poverty and inequality in income distribution have been intensified by the emphasis of the United States on maintaining its military and political supremacy in the world. Increased military spending and foreign aid have long burdened U.S. taxpayers and drained inexcusably not only the federal tax revenue but also the men, machinery, and money in the private sector that could have been diverted into the production of socially useful goods and services.

POLLUTION AND ENVIRONMENTAL PROBLEMS

Pollution in the United States, as in any other industrialized society, has for the most part arisen in the form of a negative externality of economic activity, a more or less incidental by-product excluded from corporate profit and loss statements or from personal cost-and-benefit calculations. Air and water in particular have been used as free dumping grounds by industry, agriculture, government, and the public alike.

Pollution on a massive scale is essentially a phenomenon of the postwar period. Between 1945 and 1970, the U.S. GNP increased by 126 percent, and most levels of pollution increased by at least several times that amount. The principal factors in the United States are to be found in the changing composition of output from natural to synthetic products and from nonpolluting to polluting materials and in the shift in production process from less to more polluting technology.

These commodity and industrial changes have been related of course to growth. Thus, expanded agricultural output and productivity have been made possible by the increasingly intensive use of chemical fertilizers, which are a major source of water pollution. Also, continued economic growth in the face of resource constraints has speeded the shift from natural products to synthetic substitutes. Technological innovations and the economic growth accompanying them during the past two decades have contributed to the shift in output that includes polluting substances.

The shift in technologies has taken place in a supportive socioeconomic environment. Synthetics are less costly to manufacture. Corporations profit by not treating the wastes from their production processes and by not spending money to develop pollution control technology for their production processes. Municipalities shift the burden of their wastes to downstream or neighboring communities, and individual consumers consciously or unconsciously shift the negative externalities of their activities to the community at large. Even the national government has been at fault in allowing business enterprises, local governments, and the public to continue to contaminate the open sea and rivers and lakes. Pollution has become so widespread and so deeply ingrained in the economic and social structure of the United States and many other developed countries that it is difficult to be optimistic about the prospects for its suppression and elimination within the foreseeable future.

The obvious resistance that pollution control measures would encounter from existing political and economic institutions is not the main issue here. It is, rather, the question of whether the public will be willing to forgo its current high level of material consumption or present standard of living to promote the general well-being of the community and future generations. Traditional family ties and values are breaking down in the United States and other developed countries, and thus it seems difficult to find a strong identification with and selfless devotion to present and future generations.

URBAN DECAY AND REDEVELOPMENT

Urban problems became an all-important national issue during the 1960s. Urbanization, from its beginnings in the nineteenth century, was hailed as a symbol of the economic growth, industrialization, and modernization of American society. Today, however, the same metropolis that was once considered a mecca has been deserted by many, particularly the middle class, and has been equated with crime, drugs, poverty, and visual and physiological pollution. Urban problems in the United States today seem to reflect in concentrated form social problems in the country as a whole.

In many major U.S. cities, out-migration of the white population during the 1960s was very great. For the most part, this out-migration has been in response to the in-migration of large numbers of blacks and other minorities. With such radical changes in the population mix, many large cities that began the 1960s with an average family income that was much higher than the national median had lost this differential by the end of the decade.

The large tax base and civic commitment of the middle class have been lost in this process. The cities suffer from inadequate revenues and rapidly rising costs caused by a growing demand for an increased variety of community services and rising wages for employees. Thus, the quality of essential services traditionally provided by the cities has had to deteriorate, as illustrated in public education, health and sanitation services, public safety, and transportation. The decline in the quality of such services reinforces the trend to out-migration of middle-class whites, which in turn further reduces the tax base. In meeting rising expenditures, many cities have had to initiate unpopular tax rate increases, which also contribute to the flow of the middle class to neighboring suburbs.

Money alone will not solve many of the problems found in the U.S. cities today, but strengthening city and state governments financially through federal revenue sharing on a large scale could contribute to arresting the further spread of urban problems. Many of the high-priority needs in large cities, such as public safety, environmental protection, public transportation, sewage collection and treatment, and refuse disposal, can be met more adequately. Revenue sharing will stimulate more planning of urban communities designed to serve the economic and social well-being of the population involved.

The roots of urban decay, like those of environmental deterioration, are so deeply imbedded in the dominant institutions of American society that they defy easy remedy. Short of reconstructing American society the prospects for the thoroughgoing elimination of urban problems seem dim. On the other hand, some countervailing forces clearly are present, as shown by recent improvements in mass transportation facilities, anti-pollution measures, urban redevelopment, and the amenities of living.

INSTITUTIONAL AND SOCIAL FRAMEWORK

The causes of the major economic and social problems in the United States—inflation, deteriorating balance of payments, high unemployment, poverty and inequality, environmental deterioration, and urban decay—overlap to a large extent and require steps other than the monetary and fiscal policy measures taken by the federal government. Some of the cherished American economic and social institutions and values that are being seriously questioned are those that foster and encourage unceasing economic and income growth, market competition and the survival of the fittest, unlimited material waste (nonrecycling of essential materials), and a restrained government role in any field of economic and social concern except the traditional ones of foreign policy and defense. Thrown equally into doubt are the fundamental tenets of American foreign policy—the attempt to export the very American economic and social institutions and values, which has been increasingly criticized by both domestic and foreign sources in recent years, and the commitment of U.S. money, men, and weaponry to foreign governments in the name of defending the free world from external aggression.

The steady decline through the 1960s in the relative U.S. share of the world's GNP compared with that of EC nations and Japan and in the relative U.S. military strength as compared with the Soviet Union and (increasingly) with China has been recognized by the United States. Thus, the need for grappling with domestic economic and social problems has come about. The Nixon doctrine announced in Guam in 1969 and the new economic policy of August 1971 as well as a series of subsequent economic and political measures have been the administration's response to major domestic and international economic and social problems. It is quite doubtful, as the preceding discussion has shown, that these responses will succeed in resolving the problems even temporarily. The ultimate solution will require changes in fundamental aspects of the American economy and society that are characterized by an overwhelming reliance on market mechanisms, with only a secondary role assigned to the government. This applies not only to the production of goods and services in the private sector but to the distribution of national income as well.

As can be seen, economic and social problems in the United States are due to factors inherent in the institutional and historical conditions of the society, not to accidental and short-term phenomena. In the American socioeconomic system, allocation of resources and distribution of income based on individualism and rationalism operate under a market mechanism predicated on the decentralization of decision-making authority in the form of the free enterprise system. In its favor, such a market-economy system allocates scarce private resources efficiently on the one hand and accelerates the tempo of economic growth measured by market-economy indicators on the other. It is also considered to have a desirable effect on such aspects of a society as vocational choice, diversification of consumption, and freedom of individual action.

However, under the system of remuneration based on the market evaluation of individual abilities, inequality in income distribution is an inevitable outcome. Such inequality as well as other problems emanating from it have posed major social and political issues since the second half of the nineteenth century. Within the basic framework of the market-economy system, various countermeasures have been taken for solving such problems. Included among the policies adopted after World War II were the strengthening of progressive taxation on income and inheritance and the improvement in the social security system. As a result, it might seem that the distribution of nominal income in the United States today has become more equalized.

Nevertheless, the real standard of living is not the same as the amount of nominal income; various impacts of inflation must be taken into consideration. Also, the real standard of living is affected to a large degree by the quantity and quality of goods and services provided outside the market. Social stability resulting from public policies that allow all citizens to maintain a moderate standard of living regardless of their inborn and acquired capabilities is another principal element. In this sense, the real standard of living and its patterns of distribution in any society are influenced by intangible services in the physical and social environment and public services provided directly or indirectly by various levels of basically from the inequality in such real income distribution and from the governments. The various social problems discussed previously originated social instability arising from it. Those problems, if ignored and left to grow, might bring about a breakdown in the institutional and social framework of the market economy and trigger drastic institutional reforms.

4. New Social Welfare Trends

••••••••••••••••••••••

Beginning in the early 1960s, there were signs of a policy shift in the United States, and this took a more concrete shape with the Great Society program begun by the Johnson administration in 1964. The program has been modified and expanded since that time and has required a continuous increase in government expenditures.

Since the latter part of the 1960s, measures to equalize real income distribution and restore social stability have been put into effect. The most characteristic of the new trends taking place in the United States are the various government efforts to provide services that would enable all citizens to maintain a subsistence level of living without the medium of the market. The policies are aimed at guaranteeing (at as low a level as possible, it should be added) the minimum income necessary for maintaining a basic standard of living, thereby securing social stability.

This type of welfare policy is still in embryo and appears to have retrogressed in some aspects in the course of the Nixon administration. The basic policy shift, however, seems to be permanent. The institutional and social framework of the United States has been gradually streamlined and consolidated so that the liberal economic system might continue to function smoothly without incurring serious social frictions.

CHANGES IN BUDGET OUTLAYS

A strong emphasis has been placed on programs for accelerating employment expansion and for reducing unemployment, particularly structural unemployment, a major problem for the United States. The Manpower Development and Training Act (1962) and the Economic Opportunity Act (1964) placed specific emphasis on vocational training programs for jobless young and nonwhite workers with little formal education and established such federal programs as the Neighborhood Youth Corps and the Job Corps. These programs, run by the Office of Economic Opportunity, have proved effective in raising the average income for nonwhite workers. Particularly noteworthy among such employment promotion measures in the past few years was the Equal Employment Opportunity Act (1972), whose object it is to reduce the high unemployment rate among minority groups and women. Under the provisions of this act, in order to obtain federal contracts, companies are required to employ minority and female workers as a certain percentage of total employment.

The Medicare and Medicaid systems, instituted in 1964, were epoch-making reforms in the American medical care system. In 1967, a comprehensive revision of the Social Security Act was carried out; in particular, this revision provided for an increase in the level of benefits for, as well as broadening the number of, beneficiaries under old-age, survivors, and disability insurance.

The Trade Expansion Act was enacted in 1962 to assist industrial adjustment. It provided, among other things, financial assistance to those enterprises and workers affected by a rapid increase in imports to alleviate their losses and to facilitate their shift to other industries. This system has not been sufficiently effective because of the excessively severe criteria for determining the extent of damage and the inadequacy of financial assistance. Its improvement has been called for by many, including the Commission on International Trade and Investment Policy.

The U.S. government has also taken a series of measures to prevent environmental deterioration; for example, it enacted the Clean Air Act in 1963. Under this act, various pollution control measures, including financial assistance to state and local governments, were adopted. The government also established the Air Quality Act in 1967, which identified polluted areas and established environmental criteria for all states. In its revision of this act in 1970, the government raised the clean air standards for all parts of the country and tightened regulations on automobile emissions. The Water Quality Improvement Act of 1969 was enacted to combat water pollution and provided for clean water standards and federal assistance for water-treatment facilities. The Environmental Protection Agency was created in 1970 to integrate and unify various federal measures for pollution control.

Along with the progress in such reforms, the pattern of federal budget appropriations has undergone a notable change. In fiscal 1955, the combined outlays for financing human resources development, such as education, manpower development, health and social security, social development, and residential construction, were $14.5 billion and accounted for 21.1 percent of the federal budget. However, the comparable outlay in fiscal 1974 is $130.4 billion, or 48.5 percent of the total budget. In contrast with this, the defense outlay in fiscal 1974 is only 30.4 percent of the federal budget as compared with 58.7 percent in fiscal 1955.

TRENDS IN SOCIAL WELFARE

Improvement in social welfare programs has brought a number of institutional changes as well as changes in the pattern of budgetary spending.

The budgetary outlay for social security programs increased sharply following the revision of the Social Security Act in 1967. Under the revised act, benefits under old-age, survivors, and disability insurance were increased by 13 percent, and the number of beneficiaries was increased by raising the income ceiling. In the area of public assistance, measures were adopted for increasing incentives for welfare recipients with large families to seek gainful employment; the measures allow those recipients an exemption of up to $30 per month and introduce a scheme of emergency assistance.

In order to finance such new social insurance measures, the social insurance outlay, which was $37.4 billion in fiscal 1967 and $42.7 billion in fiscal 1968, was increased to $66.1 billion in fiscal 1971. Of this 1971 total, the federal government paid 81.1 percent and the state and local governments 18.9 percent. The outlay for public assistance in fiscal 1971 was $21.8 billion. The federal government bore 60.1 percent of this and the state and local governments 39.9 percent. This represented a sharp increase from outlays of $8.8 billion in fiscal 1967 and $11.1 billion in fiscal 1968. Between fiscal 1960 and fiscal 1970, the social insurance outlay increased from $19.3 billion to $56.4 billion, and the outlay for public assistance soared from $4.1 billion to $16.5 billion. The combined total of such outlays thus increased by approximately threefold during the period. In 1972, Congress approved an amendment to the social security legislation that raised benefits by 20 percent and established a system of sliding benefits, with cost-of-living changes to be effective from 1975.

In medical care programs, both Medicare for those sixty-five and over and Medicaid for the poor, blind, and disabled were installed in 1966. Medicare is financed by premiums paid by workers, employers, and the self-employed as well as by appropriations from the federal government; Medicaid is completely financed by the federal government. Benefits under Medicaid increased from $2.5 billion in fiscal 1967 to $6.8 billion in fiscal 1971. Steady improvements have been made with the Medicare programs both for hospital and medical insurance. In fiscal 1971, a majority of the old-age population in the United States (20,580,000 persons) was covered by hospital insurance, and benefits paid under this scheme reached $5.4 billion.

Educational outlays are still unevenly distributed by regions and social groups because of the decentralized system of school administration. The pattern of cost distribution as currently shared by the federal government and state and local governments should be closely studied. In the past, the proportion of the total cost of education assumed by local governments was extremely high. In 1960, for example, the federal government paid only 6.1 percent of the total, state governments paid 36.6 percent, and local governments paid 49.2 percent. The rest came from other sources. This trend was found particularly in elementary and secondary education.

Heavy dependence by local governments on the property tax as the major source of their funds was responsible for a wide regional gap in educational outlay. The pattern of cost sharing, however, has been undergoing gradual changes in recent years. Local governments have become increasingly responsible for only the construction of educational facilities, and the federal government and state governments have begun to pay for operating expenses, including personnel. In the case of public schools, in fiscal 1972, the federal government bore 10.9 percent of the total cost; state governments, 36.5 percent; and local governments, 39.5 percent, with the rest coming from other sources.

Employment expansion—namely, the number of nonwhite and female workers employed according to the provisions of the Equal Employment Opportunity Act—is estimated, according to the budget message for fiscal 1974, to have increased to 750,000 in fiscal 1974, an enormous rise from 420,000 in fiscal 1972.

The fiscal outlays by the federal government, state governments, and local governments for housing and urban renewal projects also swelled from $1.1 billion to $3.2 billion between fiscal 1960 and fiscal 1970. Financial assistance by the federal government for urban renewal projects increased from $340 million in fiscal 1966 to $1.2 billion in fiscal 1970.

Public transportation facilities have registered gains, too. Federal assistance to state and local governments to improve urban transportation rose from $11 million in fiscal 1965 to $260 million in fiscal 1972. Although the absolute amount is small, the growth has been remarkable. Moreover, the federal government has appropriated almost $430 million for this purpose in fiscal 1974. The Urban Mass Transportation Assistance Act of 1970 requires the federal government to subsidize two-thirds of the total construction costs incurred by local governments in building public transportation facilities. A new law recently enacted by Congress permits the use of gasoline tax revenue to finance the construction of urban mass transportation facilities, a major step in improving such facilities.

NEW MANAGEMENT RESPONSES IN PRIVATE INDUSTRY

In response to the new policy moves on the part of the federal and state and local governments, private businesses and business associations have begun to seek new management philosophies and practices to replace the disproportionate emphasis on the efficiency principle. Especially noteworthy is the recent awakening among businessmen to the social responsibilities of private enterprise, although at present, there are many different interpretations of this concept. However, a consensus seems to be close in the United States that in order to survive, private enterprises must take positive steps to respond to the social pressures for corporate responsibility. On the basis of such consensus, corporations are seeking by means of a social audit to make long-range definitions of the character and scope of their social actions. Such corporate efforts seem to be bringing about some basic changes in the pattern of corporate behavior in American society.

Apart from the broader issue of social responsibility in the society at large, corporations are taking individual actions that are not profit-oriented in the short run. For example, corporate efforts for dealing with problems of environmental pollution have taken many forms. Outstanding are the projects for developing plastics that can be burned without emitting poisonous gases, perishable plastic containers, and detergents that do not contain phosphates. Also significant are the construction of mine tunnels to preserve scenic beauty and corporate efforts in developing recycling and closed-system technologies. In recent years, banks have established programs to employ members of minority groups, and some companies have made efforts to promote such employees to executive and managerial positions. An increasing number of large corporations are also making explicit in their annual reports their special interest in extending loans and providing management consultation services to smaller companies run by minority groups. In addition, many corporations are becoming active in providing financial assistance to education, extending relief to dropouts, building nursery schools, and participating in other activities beyond the scope of normal business operations.

Private businesses are thus seeking new management philosophies and practices to cope with the current "crisis," which, if mismanaged, could lead to social disintegration. This demonstrates the intrinsic merit of the adaptability of a decentralized free enterprise system. The fact that such moves have been initiated by large American corporations with great economic power and far-reaching social influence is important in evaluating the American economy and society today.

5. Prospects for the 1970s

● ●

Sɪɴᴄᴇ ᴛʜᴇ ʟᴀᴛᴇ sɪxᴛɪᴇs, definite changes have emerged in both the U.S. domestic scene and abroad. These changes are linked. Internationally, relations between the Soviet Union and China, rivals of the United States in the cold war, have changed; and both the EC and Japan have made remarkable economic progress, resulting in a relative decline in the economic position of the United States. Domestically, new problems have appeared as a result of failures in the Vietnam War policy, increased racial tensions, and so forth.

CHANGING FOREIGN POLICY

In response to such situations, the United States has abandoned the cold war policy that had long been the core of its postwar international position and has relinquished its role as the protector of the free world. The shift to a new foreign policy has been predicated on the balance of power between the United States, the Soviet Union, China, Europe, and Japan. This move can be seen in President Nixon's visits to China and the Soviet Union and in the Nixon doctrine, which emphasizes the sharing of defense responsibility by each nation.

There is, however, an inherent imbalance among these five powers. Moreover, international tensions arising from the energy and resource problems and from uncertainties in the Third World cast doubt upon whether it will be possible to implement this new foreign policy. Furthermore, the new policy is characterized by political intervention in international economic relations; for example, the United States has used its superior military and political strength to counterbalance the relative decline in its economic position, as shown in recent years by the Nixon administration. This tendency is manifest especially in U.S. relations with Japan. The 1973 International Economic Report of the President points out that since Japan is protected by the United States politically, it must show greater reciprocity in economic affairs. In negotiating with Japan, the United States has combined political issues with economic ones. To the extent that the United States must play an extremely important role in reorganizing the international economic system, this strategy may not only obstruct such reorganization but also create unnecessary international frictions.

During the cold war era, the United States was forced to allocate much of its resources to the military sector in order to sustain the unstable international political structure. The shift toward multipolarization can be expected to create a more stable world political structure, thus enabling the United States to reduce the level of its resources committed to the military sector and the proportion of its GNP going to military and economic aid. In this way, the United States will then be able to change its priorities from military affairs to seeking the solution to domestic problems. If the new policy takes root, human and material resources will be redistributed from the military sector to productive sectors in the American economy. This will contribute to reducing domestic economic and social imbalances.

CHANGING ORIENTATION IN ECONOMIC POLICY

As suggested earlier in this paper, a major share of the responsibility for many economic and social problems in the United States can be attributed to the laissez-faire principle and the market mechanism of resource allocation. However, signs of some important changes in the traditional management of the American economy can be observed.

First, public policy measures have been introduced that restrict the traditional freedom of business activities and modify the market mechanism. These government measures, such as industrial-adjustment assistance, promotion of minority employment, and pollution control, are intended to provide the basis for the fullest development of the free enterprise system by minimizing the causes of economic and social frictions.

Second, social welfare policies have had some effect. There have been improvements in public assistance, social security, medical care, job training, education, public housing, and public transportation. The Great Society program of the Johnson administration, symbolized by Medicare and Medicaid, has gradually been expanded since the latter half of the 1960s. Government expenditures for social welfare in general have thus been increasing steadily, as witnessed by the increase in federal expenditures for medical care and by the larger share assumed by the federal and state governments in the financing of education.

In order to control inflation, President Nixon has sought to hold down welfare, medical, and educational expenditures through various means, including rigorous administration of some programs, curtailment of others, and modification of medical insurance benefits. However, Congress has opposed the administration in this effort and has taken various steps to prevent the President from withholding expenditures approved by Congress. Through these and other measures, Congress is promoting welfare policies, and it can be anticipated that in the long run, welfare programs in the United States will be greatly improved.

These measures for improving welfare programs will not inhibit the fuller utilization of the potentials of the free enterprise economy. Rather, they provide the basis on which an economic system predicated upon the principles of free market mechanism might be prevented through its excesses from creating various social problems. In other words, without these measures, the potential of this market-oriented economic system cannot be fully realized, and the efficient allocation of resources cannot be achieved.

Moreover, changes are taking place within private industry. In response to the increase in the number of younger workers with new and different values, many corporations are now reexamining those methods of production and general management that tend to be solely efficiency-oriented. Such responses demonstrate that a decentralized free enterprise system is inherently capable of adjusting itself to changing circumstances. If such responses are maintained and further encouraged, the American economy will develop its potential and provide for a brighter future with fewer social tensions.

Undoubtedly, economic and social imbalances at home will not be eliminated completely during the seventies. For example, urban problems are so tied to complex issues such as racial discrimination that they cannot be solved unless serious corrective measures in housing and education are carried out. In the area of environmental problems, it would be very difficult to change the current pattern of mass production, mass consumption, and mass waste that typify the American way of life; yet changing this pattern is the key to the solution of such problems. Although inflation, which has intensified in recent years, can be kept under control to some extent through appropriate public policies and through a smoothly functioning market mechanism, it will nevertheless remain a difficult problem in the seventies because of accelerating worldwide inflation. Furthermore, the haste in which U.S. anti-inflationary policies were applied worsened the situation both at home and abroad. This was particularly true in the case of the import surcharge, which was put into effect as an emergency measure in violation of international agreements.

Nevertheless, the U.S. economy viewed in long-term perspective is moving steadily toward equilibrium. If it continues, this trend not only will restore stability to the U.S. economy and to the country's economic relations abroad but will also open new prospects. This will undoubtedly contribute to the formation of the new, stable, and equitable international economic system that the free world is now seeking.

Critique of CED's View
of the Japanese Economy
· ·

A LTHOUGH WE CONSIDER the Committee for Economic Development's study of the Japanese economy to be concise and extremely valuable, we cannot help but differ with it on a number of specific points.

The CED study evaluates the performance of the Japanese economy chiefly on the basis of the efficiency of resource allocation. Economic performance cannot, however, be judged merely on this basis. Stability, that is, maintenance of a basic standard of living for all people irrespective of individual income variation, must also be taken into account. Our comments here are thus based on a combination of efficiency and stability criteria.

We will first address ourselves to the problem of tension in Japanese-American economic relations. Then we will present our thinking on a number of specific points raised in the CED study. In this critique, we will confine ourselves to the major differences between our thinking and the views presented in the CED study; we will omit points of agreement.

WHY JAPANESE-AMERICAN RELATIONS
HAVE BEEN STRAINED

Underlying the CED report is the view that the tension in Japanese-American relations that resulted from the Nixon shocks of 1971 has not yet been relieved. Although we recognize the fact that such tension does indeed exist on the level of individual industries, we do not think that it affects the essence of Japanese-American relations. When viewed from the vantage points of both national economies, the tension can be seen to be based on short-term, localized frictions. This tension was the product of the unilateral measures taken by the United States in the late 1960s in order to cope with pronounced states of domestic and external disequilibrium.

We also concur with the belief that change in the economic environment at home and abroad gave rise to a situation in which it was imperative that Japan reappraise the principles of its economic relations with other countries. At the same time, however, we think it is necessary to reaffirm the principle of gradual realignment of international economic relations, including trade and monetary matters, on the basis of mutual understanding.

MAIN TENOR OF POSTWAR
JAPANESE-AMERICAN ECONOMIC RELATIONS

The CED paper seems to be founded on the views that Japan has unfairly maintained a balance-of-payments surplus vis-à-vis the United States by setting up various trade barriers and that Japan has been less than generous in assisting developing countries. The point is made that in the past the United States has furnished Japan with direct and indirect assistance in its economic recovery and development as well as guaranteeing its security with a nuclear umbrella and other means.

Although it is true that U.S. assistance played an important role in Japan's postwar recovery, since the 1950s the two countries have been equal partners in economic relations that have served the interests of both. In regard to trade barriers and the balance-of-payments surplus, since the 1960s Japan has cooperated in efforts to create an open international economic system by actively liberalizing trade and capital and has continued to work for equilibrium with the United States in international payments through parity adjustments and other means. Furthermore, a mere quantitative evaluation of efforts in assistance to developing countries does not seem to us to be desirable from the standpoint of the economic development of these countries.   *What is then?*

INDUSTRIAL POLICY

The CED study notes that Japanese postwar recovery through the priority production system and its subsequent rapid economic growth through heavy industrialization and promotion of exports have given rise to a variety of problems with other countries. However, emphasis on heavy industrialization and increased exports in the course of development of a country's industrial structure should not be considered peculiar to Japanese industrial policy. Rather, they are phenomena that are generally perceived in the process of economic growth of any country. Furthermore, the occurrence of problems in foreign relations in the course of the development of trade is a phenomenon inherent to free enterprise working for a better international division of labor. These problems should be solved internally through the implementation of appropriate policies of industrial adjustment. Also, these aspects of Japanese industrial policy should be considered problematic only insofar as they induce social costs and a distorted allocation of social resources from a domestic point of view.

Although it appears that a point of view based on the principle of free trade underlies CED's criticism of Japanese industrial policy, this point of view does not take into full account the costs of industrial adjustment that are an ineluctable accompaniment of free trade. Generally, there is no such thing as a free market in the overall sense of the term. Rather, the scope of tolerance of business activity and the rules applied are determined or limited by the social, historical, and natural conditions of a particular country. It therefore follows that countries differ in the substance and implementation of industrial policy. The establishment of uniform international standards would be practically impossible.

The Japanese practice of administrative guidance is an example of a special industrial policy. One can appreciate the difficulty a European or American might have in understanding this practice since legal controls provide the mainstream of industrial controls in the West. It must be remembered, however, that under certain social and historical conditions, legal controls alone are inadequate and must be supplemented by informal controls, which often improve effectiveness.

AGRICULTURAL POLICY

The CED paper contends that the Japanese policy of agricultural protection should be discarded and that imports of agricultural products should be liberalized in view of the excessive extent to which Japanese agriculture is protected and the obstacle to rational allocation of resources that this constitutes. It seems to us, however, that the role of agriculture in a national economy should be considered from a broader perspective. In order to ensure stability of supply, it is necessary to maintain self-sufficiency in food production at a certain level. Furthermore, the considerable contribution that the healthy development of agriculture makes to environmental preservation should also be recognized.

As viewed from this perspective, not all the effects of Japanese agricultural policy on the national economy to date have been adverse. For instance, the supply of rice to consumers at stable prices has indirectly worked against the rise of food prices in general. Nevertheless, the Japanese people should fully admit the inadvisability of our policy of price supports for farmers in terms of distortion of allocation of resources in agriculture and obstruction of improvement of productivity.

LIFETIME EMPLOYMENT SYSTEM

We find it difficult to agree with the CED conclusion that the lifetime employment system could have been a handicap to rapid economic growth in Japan and that if the Japanese system of employment were organized competitively, along Western lines, production would have grown more than it has. In our estimation, the lifetime employment system has been a major factor supporting rapid growth in the Japanese economy since it has given workers economic stability and a greater opportunity to make the most of their abilities.

BALANCE OF PAYMENTS

In regard to the outlook for Japan's balance of payments, the CED study presents two opposing viewpoints. One maintains that the basic surplus trend of the past will continue, and the other maintains that the factors working for a deficit are stronger. Such ambivalence is understandable in view of the fact that the study was made in October 1973, at which time the signs were not easy to read. We would like to point out, however, that as of February 1974, it seems evident that Japan's balance of payments is heading in the direction of deficits. Factors that indicate this include: the recent upsurge in the prices of petroleum, other kinds of imported energy, and raw materials; worsening international inflation; excessive liquidity occasioned by a rapid influx of foreign capital; and increased governmental expenditures as a result of the switch of policy priority to social welfare.

ECONOMIC ASSISTANCE

CED has pointed out the necessity for Japan to exert greater efforts in terms of foreign economic assistance. In connection with this, we feel that economic assistance has given rise to many sorts of problems in the recipient countries and that the mere provision of assistance is obviously not enough to ensure that the developing countries will make economic progress. It therefore behooves the giver to make a careful reappraisal of specific means of implementing such assistance programs. For instance, it should be kept in mind that economic assistance for industrialization has in the past actually enhanced inequality of income distribution and has had other adverse effects on developing countries with premodern social structures. Although we by no means reject economic assistance outright, we do believe that it is necessary to be fully aware of the fact that the kind of assistance that brings about merely quantitative expansion can have a negative impact on the economic progress of the developing countries.